Embellish
with
Embroidery

MARGARET LAND

SALLY MILNER PUBLISHING

First published in 2002 by
Sally Milner Publishing Pty Ltd
PO Box 2104
Bowral NSW 2576
AUSTRALIA

© Margaret Land, 2002

Design by Anna Warren, Warren Ventures Pty Ltd
Editing by Anne Savage
Photography by Andrew Elton, Tasty Photo and Design Pty Ltd
Photographs for Lauren and Virginia by Ricky Yanaura, Christening robe by Chuck Collins Studio
Printed in China

National Library of Australia Cataloguing-in-Publication data:

Land, Margaret.
  Embellish with embroidery.

  ISBN 1 86351 299 3.

  1. Embroidery - Patterns. I. Title. (Series : Milner craft series).

  746.44

Disclaimer
Information and instructions given in this book are presented in good faith, but no warranty is
given nor results guaranteed, nor is freedom from any patent to be inferred. As we have no
control over physical conditions surrounding application of information herein contained in
this book, the authors and publisher disclaim any liability for untoward results.

Acknowledgements

I have had a great deal of help along the way as I put these ideas together into a book. I thank the staff of The Smocking Bird in Birmingham, Alabama, for their generous donation of the beautiful skilled labour which went into the construction of the heirloom items featured in these pages. I am eternally grateful for seamstress Retha Swint, who has always been able to take my bits of embroidery and make glorious things out of them, and for the ladies of Sew So Fancy in Tuscaloosa, Alabama, who have been a source of support, encouragement and advice for many years. I called on Norma Sikes, Toni Sikes, Ann Sikes, Lydia Roper and Candi Minges for their technical advice in various areas, and I am indebted to all of them for their interest and good ideas. I must also thank Lauren Pope, Paige McLelland and First United Methodist Church of Tuscaloosa, Alabama, for the loan of their items to be photographed.

For Bob

 ontents

How to use this book

Every effort has been made to make this book as reader-friendly as possible. There is nothing worse than discovering that the project you are dying to try is explained too vaguely for you to duplicate or is far beyond your ability level. My emphasis has been on giving as much detail as possible about projects which should be within the reach of a moderately experienced embroiderer. Passing up elaborate, tricky stitches, I have searched for the simplest method to achieve a desired look. Some of the designs included here are large, but they are not overly complex. I have usually worked through the embroidery four or five times in the designing process and streamlined it as much as possible. I have tried to anticipate your questions and answer them up front. Since I know less about the construction of the articles than I do about the embroidery, I have sought out individuals more talented in that area to streamline both the construction itself and the directions for it.

What you will find in each chapter will be a common design interpreted into more than one type of embroidery and used in some fairly diverse ways. Each project has its own section with a list of materials and instructions. If a commercially available pattern is used, you will find the notions and yardages you need listed within its directions. If I have started from scratch, I list all the necessary supplies for you. There are templates for each design which you can trace onto your fabric. Any design which is too large for the book's page size has been reduced, and you will find instructions as to the proper magnification setting for a photocopier or scanner to bring it back to its original size. That original size will be the one used for the featured project. If you significantly alter it, things like yardages and ribbon width may need to be altered as well.

Read the entire section about the design before you start a project. It helps to understand how the project will be constructed before you ever cut or mark the fabric. When I have had a brainstorm about a project too late to include it in this book, I have given general directions for it at the end of the chapter under 'bonus ideas'.

There are some staple supplies I can't work without and will refer to often. You may want to consider equipping yourself with the following: graph paper, tracing paper (you can buy it on rolls at art supply stores so you aren't limited to letter-size sheets), a good mechanical pencil with 7 mm lead, a #2 (or HB) pencil for marking, as well as a blue water-soluble marker and a purple disappearing marker (get both a regular-tip and fine-point version of each), a fine-pointed chalk or soapstone marker, a ruler, a French curve and a light box or similar sort of tracing aid.

I have learned from years of teaching embroidery classes that most embroiderers are highly creative people, and they use my designs in ways I never anticipated. That is one of the basic premises behind this book: take an idea, turn it inside out and upside down, and see how many different things can be done with it. I have had a great deal of fun doing that, and I look forward to your doing so.

NOTE FOR BRITISH AND AUSTRALIAN READERS

The threads, silk ribbons and wool specified in the instructions are widely available. However, for those of you creating from 'the ground up', some of the dress patterns may be difficult to locate outside the USA. Where this is the case, you will need to substitute a similar design from another supplier, perhaps adapting it somewhat, draft your own, or simply embroider a ready-made garment. Note also that British and Australian dress sizes are not the same as US sizes.

Embroidery techniques

WORKING WITH COTTON FLOSS

DMC cotton embroidery floss comes in skeins of 6 strands twisted together. The number of strands you thread into your needle will affect the look of your stitch and will often vary depending on the scale of the design, the size of the stitches you will be making and the texture you are trying to create. No matter how many strands you choose to work with, your stitches will be smoother if you separate the threads from each other before threading your needle. To do this, cut a good working length of floss and, holding one end lightly between thumb and forefinger, pull one strand up and away from the rest. Pulling down or sideways will create a snarl, but a slow, steady, upward pull will always work. Separate all 6 strands and select the number you need to work with.

Before threading your needle, find the grain of the thread. When you put the thread into the needle's eye in the same direction as that in which the grain runs, your stitches slide through the fabric more smoothly and look sleeker; your thread doesn't wear out as quickly and you will have less snarls. This is especially important when you are making bullion stitches. To determine the proper direction in which to thread the needle, fold a length of thread in half and look at both ends. On one of them the fibres will seem to fan out and unwrap, on the other they will seem to point toward each other and hold the twist better. If that isn't readily apparent, tap lightly on both ends with a finger. Insert the end which holds the twist into your needle, and you will be stitching 'with the grain' of the thread.

A suitable all-purpose needle for your cotton floss embroidery is a #10 crewel. The eye is elongated and will accommodate 1–3 strands of floss well, yet the shaft is still slim. For bullions and French knots, try a #10 sharp. The shaft of a sharp does not taper as much as that of a crewel needle, and this uniformity of size helps make the wraps around the needle more consistent. If you are making large bullions, try a #10 milliners. It is shaped like a sharp but is longer and will hold more wraps.

Securing the thread as you start your embroidery must be done properly, without any knots which would mar the smooth surface of your finished work. There are two good methods of doing this. You can make a waste knot by tying a knot in the end of your thread and stitching through the fabric from right side to wrong side about 4 inches (10 cm) away from the point where your embroidery will begin. This knot stays in place until you are finished sewing, when you cut the knot off, thread the free length in your needle, and run it through the back of your embroidery. The other method is to make a small, shallow stitch through one or two fibres on the wrong side of the fabric at the spot where you want to begin sewing. Leaving a ½ inch (12 mm) tail, bring your needle through from the back to the front of the work, splitting the original stitch, and you are ready to start. You can snip off the tail when you finish stitching.

To secure the end of your work, you need a finishing stitch. One option is to make the same type of split stitch described for beginning your work. A second choice is to run the last of your thread through the back of your embroidery, taking care to pierce the embroidery floss but not go through the fabric.

Press your embroidery with an iron set to an appropriate temperature for the fabric. Iron all around the embroidery on the front, then turn the fabric over to press the embroidery from the back. If your work has a lot of texture to it, pad the ironing surface with a terry-cloth towel. Place a smooth pressing cloth over the towel to avoid getting an impression of the terry cloth in your fabric.

WORKING WITH SILK RIBBON

YLI silk ribbon, designed for embroidery, is widely available at fine sewing shops in packages of 5 metre lengths and is the choice for the ribbon embroidery projects in this book. The ribbon comes in a variety of widths ranging from 2 to 32 mm. All colours are available in the 4 mm width, but colour choices are limited in the other widths. Checking colour availability should therefore be one of the first steps in planning a project. If you cannot get the colour and width you need for part of your project, consider changing your plan so that you embroider the area in question with a stitch you can make with floss. In a few featured projects, where the exact shade desired was not available in the YLI line, substitutions of Bucilla products have been made. Those substitutions are noted, and you can find Bucilla silk ribbon at craft stores.

Size 24 chenille and tapestry needles are the best choices for ribbon embroidery. Both have an elongated eye, but a chenille has a sharper tip than a tapestry needle. Use the chenille needle when you need to pierce the fabric or ribbon cleanly, and use the tapestry needle when you are whipping, wrapping or weaving the ribbon and wish to avoid snagging the needle tip on the fabric or the ribbon itself. For widths above 7 mm, choose a #18 needle.

Embroidery ribbon has a tendency to wear as you stitch with it, so work with 12–15 inch (30–45 cm) lengths. When embroidering on heavy or abrasive fabrics, such as velveteen or organdie, there will be even more wear on the ribbon, and you may want to cut even shorter pieces. Using a larger needle will also help, as it creates a larger hole in the fabric that reduces the drag on the ribbon as it pulls through.

Ribbon is easily threaded into a needle, and just as easily slides out as you sew with it. You can lock your ribbon onto the needle if you have trouble with this. Thread the needle as usual, and then insert the needle tip into the ribbon about ¾ inch (18 mm) from the end of the short tail. Pull the ribbon through itself, and it will form a lock around the needle's eye. The only disadvantage to doing this is that it makes removing stitches from your work difficult.

Unlike most embroidery done with floss, there is a great deal of texture to the surface of ribbon embroidery. This means that a knot securing the stitches at the back of your work will not mar the finished surface. A simple single knot tied in the end of the ribbon will suffice. Pull it firmly to ensure that it won't come untied, but don't pull as tightly as possible, or you may end up with a knot small enough to slip through the weave of your fabric. An alternative method is to make no knot in the ribbon and to leave a ¾ inch (18 mm) tail loose on the wrong side as you make your first stitch. Holding that tail end in the proper place with one finger on the back of the work, make your second stitch through it. At the end of your stitches, tie a knot in the ribbon or run your needle through the back of a few stitches.

The single most important thing you can do in ribbon embroidery to improve the appearance of your work is to keep the ribbon straight. After pulling it through the fabric, manipulate the ribbon so as to minimise pinching and twisting. Use the straight of your needle to smooth and flatten the ribbon against the fabric before making each stitch. Twirl the needle to get rid of any twists in the strand, and use your free thumb to lightly hold the ribbon flat against the fabric as you draw it through.

Press ribbon-embroidered pieces as you would embroidery done with floss, but take care to press more gently when you are ironing over the back of the embroidery itself. An excellent aid in the pressing process is the mini-iron by Clover Needlecraft, found in the quilting section of fabric and craft stores. It has a small, flat, triangular head on the end of a wand, and heats up as an ordinary iron does. It will allow you to press the surface of small areas in between the embroidery where an ordinary iron is too large to reach. If some of your ribbon work is flatter than you like after pressing, revive it with water. Spray it on or apply with a cotton swab, soaking the ribbon but avoiding the surrounding fabric as much as possible. Then use the blunt end of a large needle or the cotton swab itself to lift and 'fluff' the problem stitches. Let the embroidery air-dry.

WORKING WITH CREWEL-WEIGHT WOOL

There are many lines of crewel-weight wool thread available, usually at needlepoint shops. Appleton wool is the one found most commonly, and is used in the projects featured here.

Crewel embroidery is closely akin to embroidery done with cotton floss. The stitches are, by and large, the same. The main difference lies in the tension. Wool is more elastic, has more body than cotton embroidery floss, and will tend to draw up the fabric even when the stitches are not too tight. Until you get a feel for the correct tension, stop and steam-press your embroidery occasionally to relax the thread and ease the pucker out of your work. If you have too much slack in the stitches, pull them a little tighter. The fuzzy body of crewel thread means that a single strand is roughly equivalent to 2 or 3 strands of floss, so be aware that stitches done in wool will look larger that those done with the same amount of cotton embroidery thread.

Finding the grain of wool thread is important because it is so loosely wrapped, compared to cotton floss, that it wears more easily. This can be aggravated by pulling it through the fabric against the grain. Follow the same procedure you used for cotton floss for determining the proper end to thread through your needle.

The wiriness of the wool thread will require a crewel needle with its longer eye in a #8 or #10. The chenille needle recommended for silk ribbon is excellent for crewel embroidery also; try a #22 or #24.

Use a good steam iron set for wool when you press your finished work. Handle as you would the other forms of embroidery described above.

Stitch glossary

STRAIGHT STITCH

Bring the needle up at A, go down again at B. Straight stitches should be fairly firm so that they lie flat on the fabric, and not too long or they may catch . they can be worked in any direction and in various lengths.

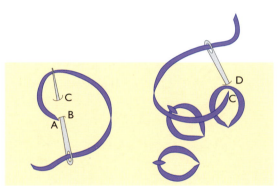

LAZY DAISY

Bring the needle up at A. Slide the needle from B. (as close as possible to A. but not actually through the same hole) through to C, taking the tip of the needle over the loop formed. Go down at D, creating a holding stitch.

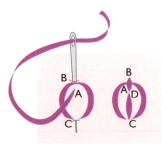

DECORATIVE LAZY DAISY

A decorative lazy daisy stitch is a lazy daisy with a single straight stitch placed inside the loop to fill in the open space.

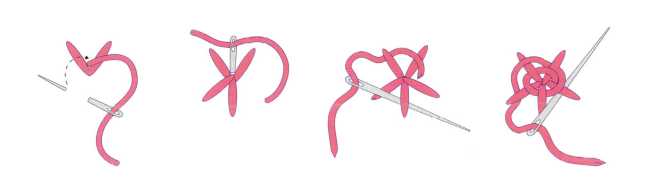

SPIDER-WEB ROSE

Work a fly stitch in matching floss to the desired size of the rose, having all three spokes of equal length. Add another spoke in matching floss each side of the Y to make five spokes in all. Bring the ribbon through from the back, working over and under the spokes. Twist the ribbon as you go, and keep it loose. Work until all the spikes are covered.

OUTLINE STITCH

Draw a line on the fabric. Bring the needle to the front at the left end of the line. Take the needle to the back at A and re emerge at B. Pull the ribbon through. Again with the ribbon below the needle, take the needle from B to C. Continue working stitches in the same manner. If the ribbon is held above the needle, this becomes stem stitch.

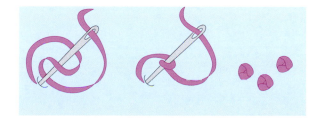

FRENCH KNOT

Bring the needle up and wrap the ribbon around it once. Holding the wrapped ribbon firmly, take the needle , holding the knot in place until the needle is pulled completely through to the back of the fabric.

JAPANESE RIBBON STITCH ALSO KNOWN AS RIBBON STITCH

Bring the needle up at A and lay the ribbon flat on the fabric. Put the needle into the middle of the ribbon at B and pull carefully through the fabric, making the edges of the ribbon curl towards the tip.

COVERED FRENCH KNOT

Make a basic French knot. Beginning near the base of the knot, make a straight stitch which covers the knot from left to right and ends on the other side Working from the top of the knot to the bottom, make a pair of close, side-by-side straight stitches,which cover the knot smoothly and create a smooth button of ribbon.

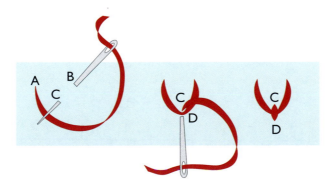

FLY STITCH

Bring the needle up at A, take the needle to the back at B and re emerge at C. Loop the ribbon under the tip of the needle and to the right. Hold the loop in place under the left thumb. Pull the needle through until the looped ribbon lies snugly against the ribbon you are pulling through. Take the thread to the back at the required distance below C to anchor the fly stitch at D.

WHIPPED STITCH

Work a line of couched thread to cover the design line. Secure the ribbon (or a new thread) on the back. Bring it to the front, just to the left of the foundation stitching. Taking the needle from right to left, slide it under the second segment of laid thread, gently pull the ribbon through. Slide the needle from right to left under the third segment, and so on, until the line has been completed.

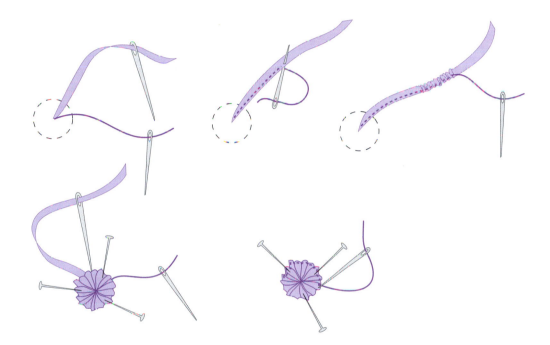

GATHERED ROSE

Pull a length of ribbon through the centre of the designated circle and pull a single strand of matching floss through close beside it. Use the floss to work a running stitch close to one edge of the ribbon. you will not need to stitch along the entire ribbon length, just enough to create the desired size base. Allow approximately 1" (2.5cm) of 4mm ribbon for each ⅛" (4mm) of diameter of the marked circle. When the necessary length of running stitch is completed, pull the floss to draw up the ribbon and slide the gathers towards the fabric. Position the gathered ribbon so that it fills the circle and secure it with pins. Draw the remaining ribbon through to the back side, knot it and clip off the excess. Use the floss to tack the gathers into position. When the rose is secure, remove the pins and tie off the floss on the back side of the fabric.

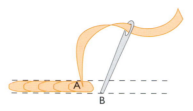

ROPE STITCH

To create the rope stitch, start with a single straight stitch. For 4 mm ribbon, each stitch should be about ¼ inch (6 mm) long; wider ribbons would require longer stitches. Use the straight of your needle to ensure that the ribbon lies as smoothly flat on the fabric as possible. The second stitch comes up from the back of the fabric and pierces the first in its upper right-hand 'corner'. Each consecutive stitch does the same to the stitch before it, working with a fairly loose tension. The result is a rope-like texture without the bulk of outline stitch.

FLOSS EMBROIDERY — OTHERWISE KNOWN AS STRANDED EMBROIDERY

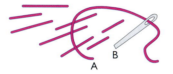

STRAIGHT STITCH

Bring the needle up at A, go down again at B. Straight stitches should be fairly firm so that they lie flat on the fabric, and not too long or they may catch . they can be worked in any direction and in various lengths.

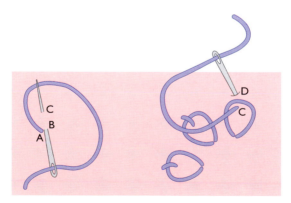

LAZY DAISY

Bring the needle up at A. Slide the needle from B. (as close as possible to A. but not actually through the same hole) through to C, taking the tip of the needle over the loop formed. Go down at D, creating a holding stitch.

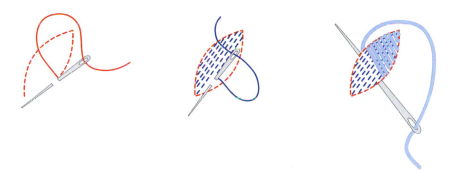

PADDED SATIN STITCH

Stitch the outline of the shape with backstitch or split stitch. Fill the shape with filling stitch making sure that the stitches run in the opposite direction to the satin stitches.

Using satin stitch and commencing at the widest section of the shape cover half the area before then covering the remaining area in the same way.

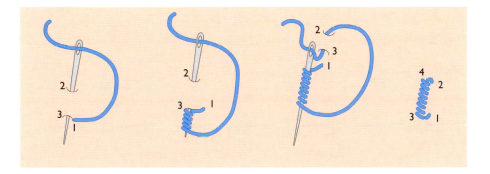

BULLION STITCH

Bring the needle up at 1 and go down at 2 leaving the loop of thread on the front of the work. Bring the needle partially through the fabric at 3. Wrap the needle with the looped thread, doing as many wraps as equals the distance between 1 and 2. Gently draw the needle through the twists and use it to hold the bullion against the fabric as you pull the thread through. Take the needle to the back again at 4 and give it a firm pull to tighten the knot.

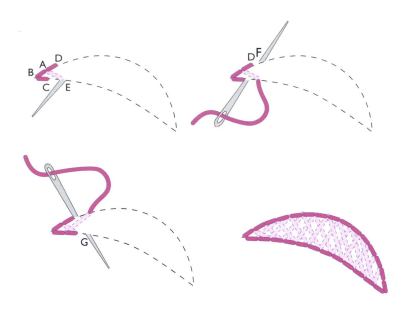

SHADOW WORK

Bring the needle up at A and take it down at B. Move across and up at C and in at B. Bring the needle out at D and back in at A, then down and across to E. Insert the needle at C and bring it out at F, re-insert at D and come out at G. Continue this sequence till finished. The diagram shows the right side of the fabric, with the crossover stitches showing through the fine fabric.

FRENCH KNOT

Bring the needle up and wrap the thread around it twice. Holding the wrapped thread firmly, take the needle down next to where it came up, holding the knot in place until the needle is pulled completely through to the back of the fabric.

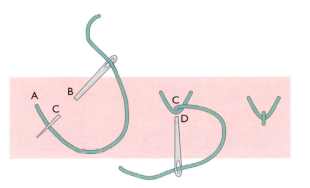

FLY STITCH

Bring the needle to the front at A. Loop the thread to the right and take the needle from B to C. Pull the thread down at D, completing the stitch.

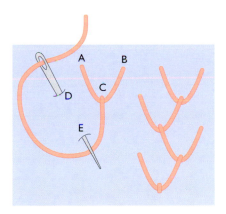

FEATHER STITCH

Bring the needle to the front at A. Loop the thread to the right and take the needle down at B and up at C. The loop is under the needle. Pull the thread through in a downward movement, holding the loop firmly with the thumb. Take needle from C to D, and up again looping the thread under needle tip.

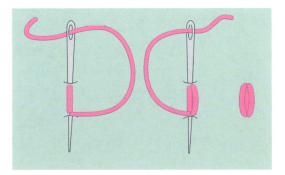

SEED STITCH (GRANITOS)

Seed stitch is two or more small straight stitches worked on top of each other to build up a seed-like texture.

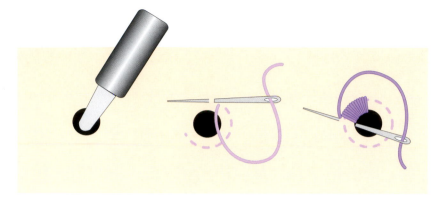

EYELET

With right side up pierce the fabric on the marked circle with an awl. Take a small running stitch just outside the hole. Pull the thread through, leaving a tail of approximately ⅛" (3mm). Work small running stitches around the circle. On the last stitch take the needle through the first stitch. Re-pierce the hole with the awl. Bring the needle and thread to the front of the work, just outside the running stitch. Take the needle through the pierced hole and bring it to the right side directly alongside the emerging thread. Pull the thread through. Holding the emerging thread under the thumb, take the needle through the pierced hole and bring to the right side alongside the previous stitch. Closely overcast the edge of the eyelet as shown. Keep turning the work to maintain consistent fanning of stitches.

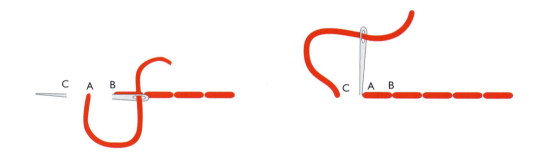

BACK STITCH

Bring the needle up at A. Take a small stitch backwards and go down at B, sliding the needle to come out at C. The distance between A and B and C, should be equal.

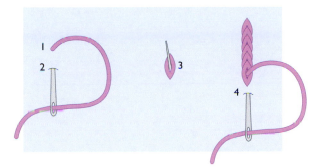

SPLIT STITCH

To create the split stitch, start with a single straight stitch. The second stitch comes up from the back of the fabric and pierces the first in the centre. Each consecutive stitch does the same to the stitch before it, working with a fairly loose tension. The result is a rope-like texture without the bulk of outline stitch.

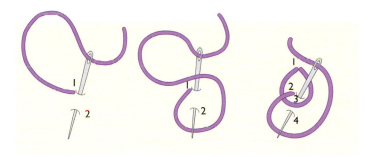

CHAIN STITCH

Bring the thread to the front at 1. Take the needle to the back through the same hole. Re-emerge at 2, ensuring the thread is under the tip of the needle. Pull the thread through until the loop begins to tighten around it. Continue pulling until the loop rests gently on the emerging thread. Take the needle from 2 to 3 to complete the first stitch, and begin the second stitch, by coming up and down at 4, and re-emerging below.

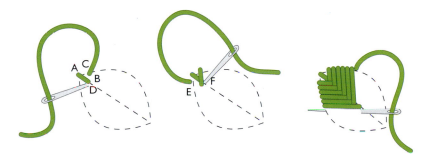

FISHBONE STITCH

Mark the shape to guide the stitches. Come up at A and go down at B along the designated centre line. Come up at C and go down at D, covering the base of the first stitch. Continue working, alternating the stitches from side to side and overlapping the base of the previous stitch, until the shape is filled.

Colour choices

For the most part, the featured projects have been worked with DMC cotton embroidery floss and perle cotton thread, Appleton crewel-weight wool thread and YLI silk ribbon. All of these can be found at numerous quality sewing and needlepoint shops. In a few cases where the desired colour could not be found in a YLI product, Bucilla silk ribbon was substituted. Bucilla products are widely available at craft stores.

A great many of the projects presented in this book are on white or ecru backgrounds. That is because it is easier to duplicate their colour schemes than those of projects with coloured backgrounds. As wonderful as colour photography is, there is no guarantee that a particular shade or tint can be duplicated or transmitted perfectly. If you want to replicate a design shown on a backdrop other than a neutral, consider the colour choices for the embroidery as suggestions only. Choose a fabric for your project which is as close an approximation of the featured colour as you can find, lay the embroidery materials on it, and make any colour changes you deem necessary. If the design calls for silk ribbon in 2 or 7 mm widths, make sure that you can get your substitute colours in the proper width.

You will often need to match DMC cotton threads with YLI silk ribbon. Consult the listings below, bearing in mind that these two products were not planned to coordinate with each other, and that dye lots for both can vary considerably. As always, let your own eye be the final guide.

COLOUR EQUIVALENTS: YLI SILK RIBBONS AND DMC COTTON THREADS

Pinks and corals		*Reds and oranges*		*Neutrals and yellows*		*Greens*		*Blues and purples*		*Browns and blacks*	
YLI	**DMC**	**YLI**	**DMC**	**YLI**	**DMC**	**YLI**	**DMC**	**YLI**	**DMC**	**YLI**	**DMC**
005	819	002	3801	001	white	18	966	009	775	004	310
006	3713	27	3328	003	white	19	562	10	519	30	3790*
007	963	28	349	12	712	20	3347	11	996	36	3772
008	776	41	350	13	3078	21	520	22	210	37	632
16	722	43	351	14	744	31	504	23	554	38	3371
17	971	48	891	15	743	32	503	44	794	52	3828
24	894	49	347	29	415	33	502	45	322	55	435
25	893	50	221	34	739	56	371	46	334	59	451*
26	761	70	3607	35	739	60	703	47	336	66	841
39	754	89	817	51	738	61	700	73	927	67	632
40	3340	92	3731	53	676	62	504	81	518	77	3830
42	3824	93	347	54	3820	63	993	82	517	79	301
68	605	108	921	57	738	64	3814	84	3685*	80	400
69	961	113	3731	58	415	71	677*	85	550*	107	3776*
76	3773	114	3721	65	3773*	72	3051	86	939*	109	920*
78	402	128	3688	119	445	74	503	90	775	140	433
83	225*	129	815	120	307	75	924	97	3756	142	3371*
87	352	130	902	121	726	94	3348*	98	3325	143	611
88	351	136	350	141	453	95	703	100	3743*	148	3828
91	893	137	355	147	676	96	701	101	210*	150	632
103	761*	146	3804	156	746	131	928	102	209	151	300
104	760	153	335*	160	950	132	598	115	3811	165	3790
105	353	159	3721	161	3774	133	3810*	116	3766		
106	722	175	347	162	452*	134	3809	117	340		
110	761	176	221	164	3782	154	504	118	3746		
111	761	180	3801			155	369	124	3756		
112	3712	181	3803			170	472	125	3753		
122	776	182	3685			171	3011	126	794		
123	956							138	823		
127	224							177	327*		
135	951							178	3042		
139	3733							179	3041		
144	3689							183	311		
145	3608							184	336		
149	402							185	823		
152	603										
157	3713*										
158	223*										
163	3727										
166	3779										
167	353										

* denotes a poor match.

Transfer techniques

Getting the design you want onto the piece of fabric you want it on is not always as simple as it would seem. Proper positioning is crucial to creating the effect you want. There is also the actual mechanical process to be worked out, wherein the colour and thickness, as well as the washability, of the fabric all have to be considered, along with the proper marking tool to use. There are several products and techniques available which might prove helpful.

The first step is to get your design out of this book and into your hands. It is too awkward to try to position the printed page underneath your fabric (and that can lead to mistakes), so either photocopy or trace the motif onto paper first. If there are magnification instructions, follow them with a photocopier or scanner to get the design to the proper size. (If you decide to make the design significantly larger or smaller, be aware that you may need to adjust ribbon widths and amounts for a silk ribbon project. Not all YLI ribbon colours are available in all possible widths, so check the colours out as well. For embroidery using cotton floss, you may need to make adjustments in the number of strands you embroider with.)

If your project is one in which you begin with fabric and a pattern, my best advice is to trace the outlines of the garment-pattern pieces you plan to embroider onto smooth, pressed, starched fabric, using a #2 (HB) pencil on those fabrics on which it will show up and coloured tracing paper for darker fabrics. Both of these markings can be difficult to remove but in this case they will be at the outside edge of the seam allowance and therefore will not be a problem. You will mark your design with something more easily removed. This way, when you finish the embroidery and wash or brush those marks away, you will still have the outline of the pattern piece on the fabric for construction purposes. If you have a large amount of fabric, it will be best to cut the pieces you are to embroider from it. Always cut them out with excess fabric around the edges, a minimum of 2 inches (5 cm) all the way around, and use zigzag stitching or a fray stopper to prevent the edges from fraying.

Where there is ample fabric available, cutting a rectangle or square piece of fabric around the embroidery tracing provides the most stability during the embroidery process.

If your fabric is washable and not too dark, use a blue water-soluble marking pen. For most ribbon embroidery, and for large-scale embroidery of any type, you will need only minimal markings to indicate the size and position of the various stitches, so the regular-tip marker is suitable. For very small motifs or shadow embroidery, where precision marking is crucial to a good final product, use a fine-tip marker. Sometimes a new pen will be so full of ink that it bleeds out too much as you mark with it. Leave the cap off for a few hours, and exposure will take care of the problem. To remove markings when the embroidery is completed, flush the fabric with water. Either let water run through it for 10–15 seconds, or swish it vigorously in a container of water. Let it air-dry, and if you see blue ink returning, rinse it again. The ink can always be removed, but it is sometimes stubborn and doesn't show up until the fabric is totally dry. In some cases residual ink has seemed to react to heat when a fabric was ironed, and left a beige stain, so be sure that there is no blue visible before you do any pressing.

For a dark fabric, use a sharp chalk pencil or a soapstone pencil. Both of them can be removed with a clothes brush. They don't allow you to be as precise as a marking pen does, but they do show up and are harmless to your fabric.

If you are planning to embroider on an unusual synthetic or a fine wool or silk whose washability is questionable, ask for cleaning instructions at the fabric store where you purchase it. I also recommend doing your own testing. Some wools and silks which require dry-cleaning can handle water. Spray a small corner with water and see how the fabric reacts and how it looks after drying. Mark on it with a water-soluble marker and rinse to see if the marks disappear without leaving a trace. Iron the area afterward to make sure that heat does not bring the markings back up. If you can't use that type of pen, test a purple disappearing marker. Its marks disappear with exposure to air in 48 hours or so (the time seems to vary a good bit, probably depending on the surface finish of the fabric, but the marks do disappear). Check to see if it leaves any trace, both before and after pressing. If you decide to use this type of pen, be prepared to mark only as much of the design as you have time to embroider so that you are not repeatedly redrawing the unfinished parts. Your last option in these cases is the chalk or soapstone pencil. The chalk is available in colours for use on pale fabrics.

To best position the design on the project, I recommend making a tracing-paper copy of the necessary pattern piece, or the outline of the object on which you will be sewing if you will be embroidering on a finished item—the front of a purse or the corner of a blanket, for example. Mark a centre line and any other landmarks, such as seam allowances, trims or fasteners, on the tracing paper. Place that over your design template and align those markings with the design's centre line and any other relevant points detailed in the placement instructions. Trace the design onto the tracing paper, and you now have a completed plan for positioning your design.

The easiest method of transfer is tracing, and the greatest aid to that is a light box. I have one which was built for me, but there are other options. There are small plastic ones available in the art departments of many toy stores. If you have a glass-topped breakfast table or coffee table, you can create one for yourself. Put an inexpensive gooseneck lamp underneath the table, shine the light upward, and you have a light box. If you want to build one, you will need a wooden box deep enough to hold a round fluorescent light fixture and a frosted glass top. I like to tape the paper template to the glass and hold the fabric in place over it with pins or weights. If my template is drawn in pencil, and my fabric and/or embroidery colours are pale, I tape a piece of medium-weight clear plastic film over the template to prevent pencil markings from rubbing off on the back of the fabric and soiling it or the embroidery thread. The clear film is available at craft stores.

If you are transferring the design onto an opaque or dark fabric and therefore can't trace it, you may be able to outline it. Photocopy or trace the motif onto heavy paper or cardboard, making as many copies as you will need to cover the embroidery area. Cut them out, pin them to the fabric, and mark around the edges. Then refer to the template for the finer details. You can mark some of those details inside the outline you made or freehand them as you go. This method works best with simple forms.

Dancing bows with a distinctly Asian touch form one of the most versatile motifs in this collection. A unique decorative touch for garments, suitable for kindergarteners as well as adults, this design can also add an exciting accent to a wide range of home decors. The highly stylised bows can be embroidered in several ways—silk ribbon, shadow work or satin stitch—depending on the look desired and the weight of the fabric being embroidered. The items featured here are worked on fabrics as diverse as velveteen, georgette and piqué.

TRANSFER

Use template A (page 33) for shadow work and satin stitching. Use template B (page 34) for ribbon embroidery. Each contains several different bows, and it is recommended that an equal number of each be scattered at random over the surface of the embroidered item. Planning the placement is important. Trace or photocopy each bow several times. Cut them out and pin them in place as you like on the finished item or on the pattern. When satisfied with your arrangement, trace each bow into place onto the fabric. Clear outlines of template A are necessary for working in satin stitch or shadow work. Template B for ribbon embroidery can be traced if your fabric permits, but can also be easily freehanded. Just leave the numbered paper outlines in place, mark the end of each arm of the bow with dressmaker's chalk or purple disappearing marker to indicate the position of the stitches, and proceed to embroider one at a time, removing each paper outline as you work and referring to the template as a guide.

EMBROIDERY

For the shadow-stitched and satin-stitched bows, use a single strand of floss. Work the two small centre segments first, and then embroider the other sections, starting at the narrow end of each and working outward.

The steps for creating the ribbon-embroidered interpretation are presented in a diagram with template B on page 34.

GIRL'S DRESS
ILLUSTRATED ON PAGE 31

Materials
McCall's dress pattern #2074, view B,
  US size 12
ecru double georgette
DMC cotton floss
  #503, green
  #758, pale terra cotta
  #3820, gold
  #841, khaki
template A

Special embroidery notes

Sixty bows are scattered over the front and back of the child's dress. Placement was done according to the transfer instructions, with a wider spacing between bows at the bodice level and a gradually closer spacing as you work your way down the skirt of the dress to the hem. Trace the bows carefully and clearly and embroider as directed in shadow stitch. A light spray of water did not harm the polyester georgette used for this dress and effectively removed the water-soluble markings. Test your fabric before marking it.

Construction notes

Follow garment pattern instructions.

ROUND-COLLARED SUNDRESS
ILLUSTRATED ON PAGE 32

Materials

Chery Williams 'basic square yoke dress' pattern,
  view 3, sleeveless, unsmocked
½ yd (0.5 m) Swiss piqué
navy and white stripe cotton chintz
navy piping to match fabric
round collar pattern
DMC cotton floss, #336, navy (this may vary—
  choose the best match for your fabric)
template A

Adrienne bows in satin stitch, shadow work and ribbon embroidery
Opposite Adrienne girl's dress in ecru double georgette, embroidered in cotton floss (see page 29)

30

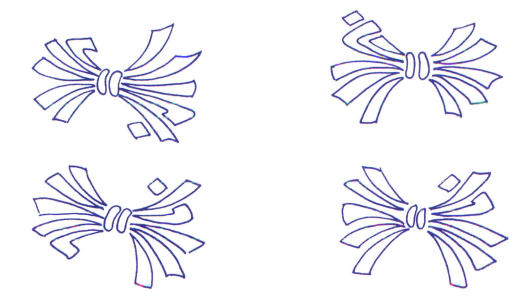

Adrienne: Template A
For shadow embroidery or satin stitch, both worked with 1 strand of floss

Special embroidery notes

Place bows from template A at random on the collar pattern (9 bows were used on a US size 6 collar). Trace the pattern piece and bows onto your fabric. The bows should be cleanly drawn in order to get the best embroidery result. Embroider as directed in satin stitch in a single strand of navy floss.

Construction notes

The Chery Williams dress pattern used here does not include the desired collar but was chosen because it has a high yoke which hits at mid-armhole and can be completely hidden by a large round collar. Any pattern for such a collar can used, with its neckline redrawn to match up with the dress neckline. The collar edge is finished off with navy piping. Follow the pattern directions for the construction of the dress.

Opposite Adrienne round-collared sundress with satin-stitched bows on collar (see page 30)

Adrienne: Template B
For ribbon embroidery

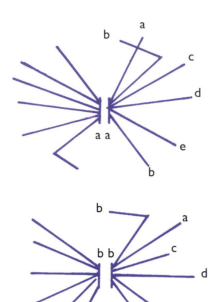

Colour guide
a = #148, bronze
b = #51, beige
c = #143, sepia
d = #56, olive
e = #71, champagne

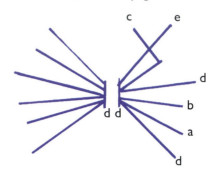

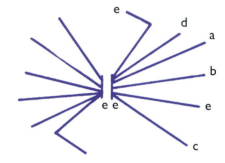

Steps in working ribbon-embroidered bow

↓ ↓

a: Begin with the two centre segments, making two short straight stitches.

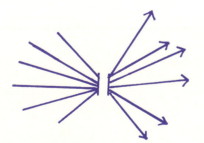

b: Each long straight stitch in the body of the bow is threaded under these centre stitches.

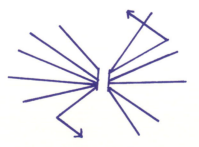

c: Form a bent arm by making a second straight stitch at an angle to the first.

VELVETEEN PILLOW
ILLUSTRATED BELOW

Materials
19 inch (18 cm) square pillow with removable
 velveteen cover
YLI silk ribbon (4 mm), 1 pack each:
 #148, bronze
 #51, beige
 #143, sepia
 # 56, olive
 #71, champagne
template B

Special embroidery notes
Open the zipper, remove the pillow form, and transfer 13 bows from template B by the freehand transfer method. The ribbon-embroidered bows are larger than those worked in floss and have 6 arms rather than the 5 of the floss bows. The colours are assigned at random on the template. Even if you choose another set of colours to complement your pillow, the same plan can be used; just assign the labels a, b, c, d and e to the new colours.

Adrienne velveteen pillow with ribbon-embroidered bows (see this page)

'Aislinn' is a playful informal alphabet with lower-case letters formed from flowers. You can make the flowers with a variety of stitches so this design is easily worked by a beginning embroiderer, but is rewarding to the experienced stitcher as well. The three featured projects illustrate that wonderfully. In the first, bullion roses form a young girl's name across the surface of a boudoir pillow. A delicate heirloom-smocked dress featuring a silk ribbon monogram centred on its front panel is the second project. The third is a hemstitched piqué blanket decorated with a riotously colourful alphabet, worked in the easy-to-do lazy daisy stitch and suitable for a child of either sex, possibly the cutest baby gift ever.

TRANSFER

Neatness counts when it comes to spelling out monograms and names. Traditionally, there are two ways to make a full-name monogram. One is to use the three initials in the same size and in the order in which the names occur, the same method used for spelling out a name. The other method is to centre a larger family name initial and place the others on either side of it. Whichever style you choose, it is important that the letters are lined up evenly and straight. The best aid in doing this is graph paper. To write a name or a monogram in the first style, trace the letters you need from the alphabet template along a base line on graph paper, spacing them as you feel they look best. You will notice as you position them that they may not be identical distances apart. This is because your eye is inclined to prefer visual balance over mathematically perfect spacing, and in this case, what looks right, is right. For the second style, mark a base line on the graph paper and a top line above it to indicate

the height of the smaller letters. Use a photocopier or scanner to create a larger family name initial (set the enlarger on 115 per cent for this particular project). Trace that letter first, positioning it so that it extends an equal distance above the height line and below the base line. Then trace the smaller letters on the base line on either side, relying on your eye again for their positioning.

When all the letters are drawn, fold the graph paper in two vertically so that the grid lines match up and the beginning of the first letter is aligned with the end of the last letter. Crease the paper, open it, and mark the crease with your pencil. This crease line is rarely down the middle of your middle letter, so don't let that concern you. Next, fold the paper across the letters so that the tops of the letters are even with the bottoms. Again, crease, open and mark. Where the two crease lines intersect is the centre of the motif. You will find the midpoint of whatever you are transferring the design onto by folding it in

Aislinn boudoir pillow, the name embroidered in bullion roses in cotton floss

halves the same way. When you align the point on the paper with that on the fabric, you will have your letters centred. Make sure your base line is straight, and you are ready to transfer. A water-soluble marker may be used to mark all three projects.

EMBROIDERY

The purchased pillow was obviously embroidered after it was constructed, and the silk ribbon monogram on the dress could be as well. This, however, would entail washing the entire garment after completing the work, so you may prefer to embroider the front panel on the fabric before the construction is done. The blanket must be embroidered before it is constructed.

BOUDOIR PILLOW
ILLUSTRATED ABOVE

Materials
rectangular flanged boudoir pillow
DMC cotton floss:
   #524, green
   #760, terra cotta pink
   #3713, lighter pink
templates A, B and C

Note Any two shades of your choice can be substituted for the pinks, along with a complementary green.

Special embroidery notes

The flowers here are bullion roses. Since they tend to be irregular in shape, the placement of the leaves around them may vary somewhat from the template. It is a good idea to embroider all the roses first, then go back and fit the foliage around them, keeping your stitches within the general outline of the letter. The bow embellishment fits on the first and last letters of the name and can be attached to any letter of the alphabet. The addition of the darker outline-stitch trim along one edge helps emphasise the twists of the ribbon and gives your bow some depth. As a final touch, the same darker floss is threaded through the hemstitching at the inner edge of the flange. Use all 6 strands of the floss for this and secure the thread on the back of the work, inside the envelope opening, before you begin and when you finish.

Aislinn heirloom dress for a baby (see page 39)

HEIRLOOM DRESS
ILLUSTRATED ON OPPOSITE PAGE

Materials

Chery Williams 'lacy bishop, bonnet and slip
  pattern', view 1
Terry Jane smocking plate, 'lacy bishop and lacy
  bonnet'
DMC cotton floss:
  ecru
  #739, deeper ecru
YLI silk ribbon, #34 (2 mm), 1 pack
YLI silk ribbon, #34 (4 mm), 1 pack
templates A and D

Special embroidery notes

Follow the stitch guide on template D. The bows here are done in shadow work while the roses are worked in silk ribbon. Use the 2 mm ribbon to form the roses; the 4 mm ribbon is threaded through the beading outlining each panel and decorating the sleeves of the dress.

Construction notes

The smocking is done with 2 strands of #739 floss according to the bishop dress instructions in the smocking plate. Small spider-web roses just like those in the monogram are substituted for the flowerettes the pattern calls for, and the lazy daisy leaves are done in 2 strands of floss like those on the monogram. Follow dress pattern instructions to assemble the dress after the smocking and embroidery are completed.

If the Terry Jane smocking plate is not available, you may substitute any bishop-dress design with the appropriate number of rows of smocking for your size dress. Check the dress pattern instructions for that number.

ALPHABET BLANKET
ILLUSTRATED ON PAGE 40

Materials

1⅓ yd (1.25 m) Swiss piqué (the fine soft Swiss fabric
  is worth the extra cost for this project)
templates A and E
DMC cotton floss:

#210	#340	#352	#368	#369	#444
#554	#605	#613	#703	#704	#722
#742	#745	#760	#772	#794	#809
#913	#989	#3078	#3326	#3348	#3608
#3609	#3766	#3819	#3822	#3825	

Special embroidery notes

Before transferring the alphabet to your fabric, the blanket should be blocked off on the piqué by pulling threads (see layout diagram below). For a 36 inch (90 cm) square finished blanket, pull threads to delineate a 44 inch (112 cm) square. Cut along those lines, zigzag the raw edges, and turn them under ¼ inch (6 mm) all the way around. Pull a second set of threads 4 inches (10 cm) in from all four sides. With a marking pen and a ruler, draw a square which is 3¾ inches (9.5 cm) inside the four pulled thread lines. Trace the alphabet around one corner, centring the template between the pulled thread lines and the marker lines.

Layout for Aislinn alphabet blanket

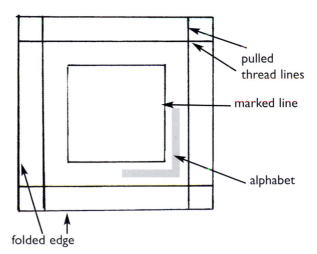

pulled thread lines

marked line

alphabet

folded edge

Aislinn alphabet blanket, embroidered in colourful lazy daisy flowers in cotton floss on Swiss piqué (see page 39)

The lazy daisy flower petals, the French knot centres and the lazy daisy leaves are all small but are done using 2 strands of floss, which gives the embroidery a wonderful texture. The colours of the letters begin with a peach and work their way through the colour spectrum twice. There are 13 colour combinations, and each one is used twice. Follow the chart on the right

Construction notes

After the embroidery is completed, hemstitch along the marker line. Fold the edges of the blanket back along the pulled thread line, and mitre the corners at the back. Slipstitch the folded edge to the hemstitching on the blanket's back.

Letters	Petals	Centres	Leaves
a, n	#3825	#722	#3348
b, o	#352	#3609	#704
c, p	#605	#745	#772
d, q	#3608	#722	#704
e, r	#554	#3078	#3348
f, s	#340	#3822	#368
g, t	#794	#210	#3348
h, u	#3766	#3822	#703
i, v	#913	#3326	#3348
j, w	#704	#809	#369
k, x	#3819	#760	#368
l, y	#444	#809	#989
m, z	#742	#613	#368

Detail of Aislinn alphabet blanket embroidery

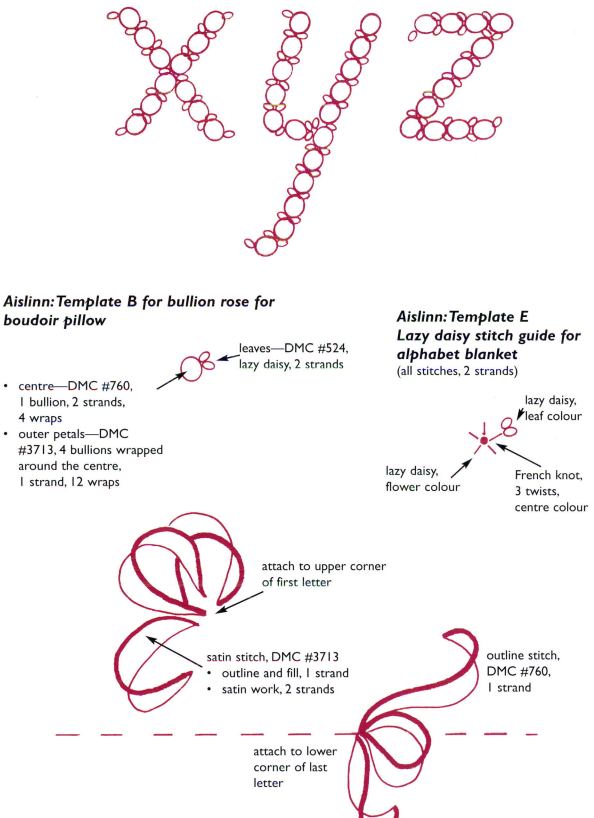

Aislinn: Template B for bullion rose for boudoir pillow

leaves—DMC #524, lazy daisy, 2 strands

- centre—DMC #760, 1 bullion, 2 strands, 4 wraps
- outer petals—DMC #3713, 4 bullions wrapped around the centre, 1 strand, 12 wraps

Aislinn: Template E
Lazy daisy stitch guide for alphabet blanket
(all stitches, 2 strands)

lazy daisy, leaf colour

lazy daisy, flower colour

French knot, 3 twists, centre colour

attach to upper corner of first letter

satin stitch, DMC #3713
- outline and fill, 1 strand
- satin work, 2 strands

outline stitch, DMC #760, 1 strand

attach to lower corner of last letter

Aislinn: Template C for boudoir pillow

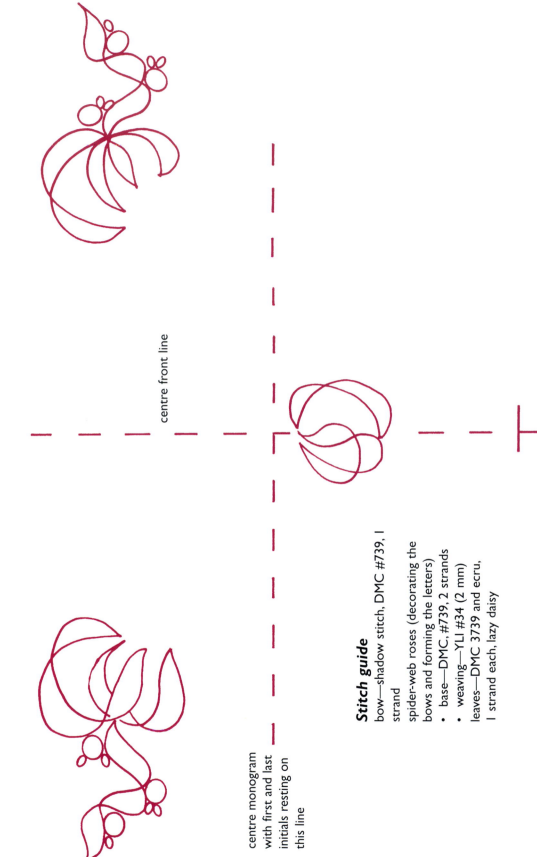

Aislinn: Template D for heirloom dress

centre front line

centre monogram with first and last initials resting on this line

Stitch guide

bow—shadow stitch, DMC #739, I strand

spider-web roses (decorating the bows and forming the letters)
• base—DMC, #739, 2 strands
• weaving—YLI #34 (2 mm)

leaves—DMC 3739 and ecru, I strand each, lazy daisy

44

Blair

Dancing fans with colourful streamers drift across the surface of a variety of items embellished with the 'Blair' design. They look right at home on a sophisticated hot pink satin sheath, and certainly can enliven an heirloom dress, as a pale pink linen creation trimmed in wide Cluny lace illustrates. The large-scale shadow-embroidered version of the same design even makes something extraordinary out of a simple shower curtain. You'll find lots of uses for this elegantly feminine motif.

TRANSFER

The shadow-work version of 'Blair' needs to be traced carefully to get the best possible result in your embroidery. The ribbon-embroidery interpretation need not be as precisely transferred and can be outlined in chalk if your project is a dark or opaque fabric, such as the satin dress featured. This entails tracing or photocopying several of each of the 5 fans (24 fans were used to decorate the front of the US adult size 6 dress pictured) onto heavy paper and cutting them out. Pin them into place on the item to be embroidered and trace around each one with chalk. Then, using your template as a reference and following the stitch guide, you can freehand the embroidery.

EMBROIDERY

The framework of the fans is worked in 2 strands of floss whether they are done in shadow work or ribbon embroidery. There are 10 plumes per fan in the ribbon-embroidered version. The larger-scale shadow-embroidered fans have 8 plumes per fan and are done with 2 strands of floss. See the stitch guide illustration for each version.

SATIN SHEATH DRESS
ILLUSTRATED ON PAGE 46

Materials

sleeveless satin sheath dress in hot pink
YLI silk ribbon (4 mm, 1 pack each—estimate 15 fans
  per 5 m pack):
    #11, turquoise
    #18, green
    #20, olive green
    #85, purple
    #102, lavender
    #133, deep seafoam
DMC cotton floss:
    #210, lavender
    #340, periwinkle
    #400, deep rust
    #471, spring green
    #780, ginger
    #841, tan
    #913, mint green
    #3609, pink
    #3772, copper
templates A and B

Blair: Template A for satin sheath dress
Ribbon-embroidered fan stitch guide

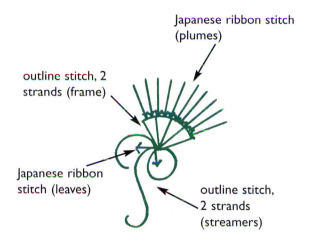

Japanese ribbon stitch (plumes)

outline stitch, 2 strands (frame)

Japanese ribbon stitch (leaves)

outline stitch, 2 strands (streamers)

Special embroidery notes
An unadorned purchased dress was the basis for this project, but it would be simple to make your own sleeveless sheath. The embroidery can be marked and worked on the dress front before the dress is assembled or, as in this case, on the finished garment. If you are working on a finished dress with a lining, make sure to separate the dress from the lining; you don't want your stitches to go through both layers. Follow the transfer instructions using the 5 fans in template B. Referring back to template A, embroider the frames for each fan first in outline stitch with 2 strands of floss, and then the plumes. The plumes are made of 1 Japanese ribbon stitch each, worked 'upside down'—that is, from the outer edge down toward the spokes of the frame. The streamers should be done next, using 2 strands of floss in an outline stitch. Finish with the 2 straight stitches of ribbon which form the green leaves at the base of each frame.

CHILD'S HEIRLOOM DRESS
ILLUSTRATED ON PAGE 48

Materials
Children's Corner pattern, 'Lily', view C
pale pink linen
matching pink batiste for slip bodice
tatted insertion
3¼ inch (9.5 cm) wide Cluny lace
3 mm pearls (60 for child's US size 10 dress)
DMC cotton floss:
   #598, aqua
   #745, pale yellow
   #3032, khaki
   #3716, pink
   #3747, light periwinkle
YLI silk ribbon (4 mm), 1 pack each:
   #003, white
   #009, pale blue
   #100, pale lavender
   #156, pale yellow
Bucilla ribbon (4 mm), #240, avocado green, 2 packs
template D and detail C

Special embroidery notes
Follow detail C for the placement of the motif down the centre of the bodice. Template D is the repeat for the fancy band in the skirt and on the sleeves. The embroidery can be worked before or after the garment is completed. A single pearl is attached with white sewing thread at the base of each fan.

Construction notes
Some modifications were made to the 'Lily' pattern to create the dress you see in the photo. The fullness at the tops of the sleeves was taken out for a closer-fitting silhouette. At the marking for a line of lace insertion on the sleeves and the skirt, I substituted the tatted insertion plus a 2 inch (5 cm) wide embroidered fancy band and

Opposite Blair satin sheath dress trimmed with a multitude of fans embroidered in silk ribbon and cotton floss

fan #1

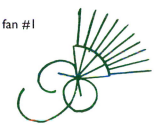

fan #3

fan #5

fan #2

fan #4

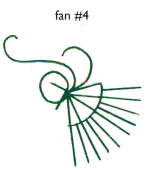

Blair: Template B for satin sheath dress

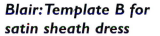

Colour guide for template B

	YLI silk ribbon (plumes)	DMC floss (frame)	DMC floss (streamers)
fan #1	#11	#780	#3609
fan #2	#18	#400	#340
fan #3	#85	#841	#913
fan #4	#102	#841	#471
fan #5	#133	#3772	#210
all leaves—YLI #20			

the wide lace edging. This change eliminates the hem on the sleeve and the skirt. You will need to adjust the lengths of those pieces to accommodate the changes. The bodice lining was omitted on both the overblouse and the slip for a lighter look. The neck and armhole openings of the slip can be finished by whipping or shell-stitching. For the bodice neck and centre back opening, 2 inch (5 cm) wide facings were cut from the dress fabric using the bodice front and back pattern pieces as guides.

Bonus colourway

Pale tints for use on a white dress:

YLI ribbon (4 mm) #005 pink fan with
  DMC #3753 aqua cord
YLI ribbon (4 mm) #83 mauve fan with
  DMC #772 green cord
YLI ribbon (4 mm) #90 blue fan with DMC #3779
  salmon cord
YLI ribbon (4 mm) #100 lavender fan with
  DMC #3689 pink cord
YLI ribbon (4 mm) #131 seafoam fan with
  DMC #945 peach cord
YLI ribbon (4 mm) #135 peach fan with
  DMC #3747 periwinkle cord
YLI ribbon (4 mm) #156 yellow fan with
  DMC #3743 lavender cord
YLI ribbon (4 mm) #155 for leaves
DMC cotton floss #644 for fan frames

Opposite Blair child's heirloom dress

line b

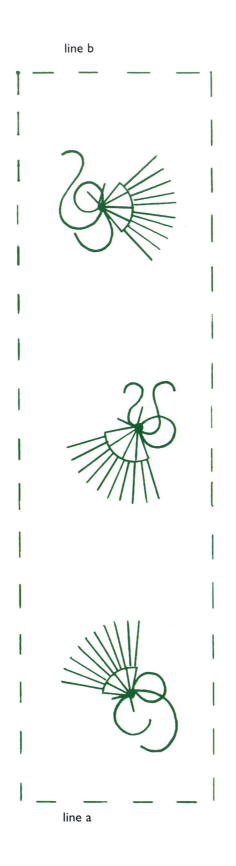

Blair: Template D for child's heirloom dress

line a

The 4 colourways are repeated through the 3 fan shapes in numerical order to make the pattern more lively

Colour guide for Blair template D and detail C

fan frames—DMC floss #3032
leaves—Bucilla silk ribbon #240

	YLI silk ribbon (plumes)	DMC floss (streamers)
fan colourway #1	#003	#598
fan colourway #2	#009	#3716
fan colourway #3	#100	#745
fan colourway #4	#156	#3747

3 mm pearl at the point of each fan frame

Detail C of embroidered fans on bodice of Blair child's heirloom dress

ORGANDIE SHOWER CURTAIN

Materials
hemstitched white organdie shower curtain,
  approx. 72 inches (185 cm) square
DMC cotton floss:
  #209, lavender, 2 skeins
  #340, periwinkle, 2 skeins
#368, medium green, 2 skeins
#597, aqua, 2 skeins
#703, bright yellow-green, 2 skeins
#799, blue, 3 skeins
#809, bright blue, 4 skeins
#913, clear green, 2 skeins
#3782, khaki, 2 skeins
templates E and F

fan #3

fan #2

fan #1

Blair: Template E
Tracing guide for shower curtain panel

Special embroidery notes

Template F includes three colour plans for the shower curtain design and template E shows the layout of the fans for one panel. There are six panels in all, and only every other one will be embroidered. For variety's sake, turn the template upside down for the middle panel. The shadow embroidery is done with 2 strands of floss, as are the outline-stitch streamers. Start each fan at one top corner and work the shadow embroidery diagonally across the entire space of the 10 plumes, as indicated in the diagram below. Use the same colour in a back stitch to fill in the lines which delineate the individual segments. Weave #809 floss, using all 6 strands, through the hemstitching, over and under 3 spaces at a time.

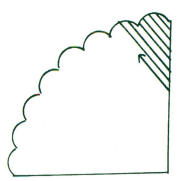

Direction of stitches for shadow-embroidered fan on shower curtain

Construction notes

No construction is necessary for a purchased shower curtain. If desired, one can be constructed from any basic shower curtain pattern, using large entredeux, faggotting or hemstitching to create six panels of equal size.

Bonus ideas

Reduce the shadow-work design to the size of the ribbon embroidery templates and scatter the fans across a tea-time tablecloth in colours to complement a china pattern. Because they will be so much smaller than the fans on the shower curtain, use a single strand of floss for all the embroidery on this project.

Place a fan in one corner of each of a set of matching napkins to create a unique gift.

Embroider a sheer linen table set in white, ecru and pale green for a truly special bridal shower.

Blair: Template F for shower curtain
Stitch guide for shadow-embroidered fans

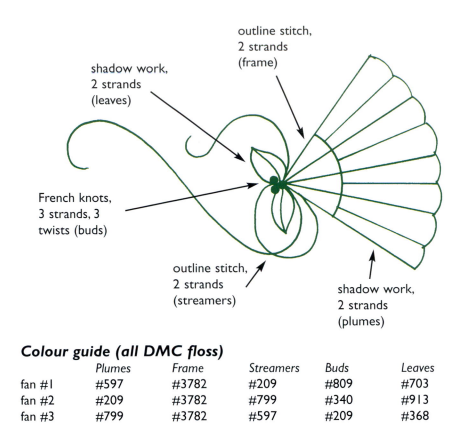

outline stitch,
2 strands
(frame)

shadow work,
2 strands
(leaves)

French knots,
3 strands, 3
twists (buds)

outline stitch,
2 strands
(streamers)

shadow work,
2 strands
(plumes)

Colour guide (all DMC floss)

	Plumes	Frame	Streamers	Buds	Leaves
fan #1	#597	#3782	#209	#809	#703
fan #2	#209	#3782	#799	#340	#913
fan #3	#799	#3782	#597	#209	#368

Probably the simplest pattern in this collection, 'Carolyn' has a lot to offer to any embroiderer, even a beginner. Clusters of spiky, aster-like blooms in groupings of one, two or three are easy to scatter across the surface of almost anything to give it a quick and easy facelift. The design is offered in silk ribbon and in traditional floss on items as diverse as a linen dress, a child's fleece jacket and hat, and a velveteen bag.

TRANSFER

Transferring this design onto the white linen dress is easily accomplished by tracing with a water-soluble marker. Template A offers a repeat of the pattern and directions for enlarging it to cover any size garment. If your dress has darts, as this one did, stitch them in place first so that your embroidery can extend over them if necessary. If your dress will have a lining it may be best to embroider the garment pieces before they are assembled. If there is no lining you may do the embroidery before or after construction.

Transferring the design onto dark opaque fabrics, like the blue fleece of the jacket or the black velveteen of the purse, is done differently. Choose the appropriate template and photocopy or trace it onto heavy paper or poster board. Cut out the large circles. Pin the paper in place over the item to be embroidered and mark the circles using a fine-pointed chalk pencil or soapstone marker. Mark the positions of the leaves. Draw a smaller circle inside each larger one to help you position the two rings of stitches. If any of the chalk shows after you finish your embroidery, remove it with a clothes brush.

EMBROIDERY

Although the ribbon-embroidered version of 'Carolyn' looks quite different from the floss one, they have one thing in common: they are both composed of two rings of overlapping stitches. On both of them you will embroider the outer circle first. Make the required stitches from the edge of the inner circle to the edge of the outer circle first. The second set will begin from the centre and reach just past the edge of the inner circle to overlap the base of the bottom ring of stitches. There will be half as many stitches in the second layer as there were in the first (see diagram below).

Working the aster-like flowers for 'Carolyn'

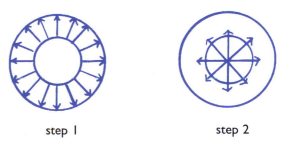

step 1   step 2

LINEN SHEATH DRESS
DETAIL OPPOSITE

Materials

Butterick pattern #3053, view A
white linen
YLI silk ribbon (4 mm):
    #009, baby blue, 5 packs
    #31, green, 2 packs
    #97, aqua, 5 packs
    #115, seafoam, 5 packs
    #125, clear blue, 5 packs
YLI silk ribbon (7 mm):
    #009, 3 packs
template A

Note The ribbon amounts listed are those required for a child's US size 14 dress embroidered only on the front. The ribbon requirements for your project may vary from this depending on the garment size. As a general rule you can plan to get 7 flowers, 40 leaves or 20 dots from each 5 m package of ribbon.

Special embroidery notes

For the size 14 child's dress, trace or photocopy six copies of template A from page 58. For larger garments, you will need more copies, but the process will be the same. Tape three of the copies together with line ab of one copy abutting line cd of the next. Tape the remaining copies to the first three with lines ac abutting lines bd to create a large square (see diagram opposite). You will now have an area of the design repeat large enough to cover the large pieces of your pattern. Trace the outlines of the dress front and dress back from the garment pattern onto the linen with a #2 (HB) pencil. Cut them apart, leaving at least a 2" (5 cm) margin of excess fabric all the way around the outlines. Finish the raw edges to prevent fraying, make any necessary darts, and insert the zipper. Position the fabric pieces over the large pattern repeat you have created and trace the design onto the fabric.

To embroider, follow the stitch guide. The Japanese ribbon stitch blossoms will have 16 petals in the larger, bottom layer, and 8 petals in the top layer of stitches. The covered French knots, which can be placed randomly, require 1 knot, 1 horizontal cover stitch, and 2 overlapping vertical stitches.

Construction notes

Follow pattern instructions.

Layout for linen sheath pattern repeats

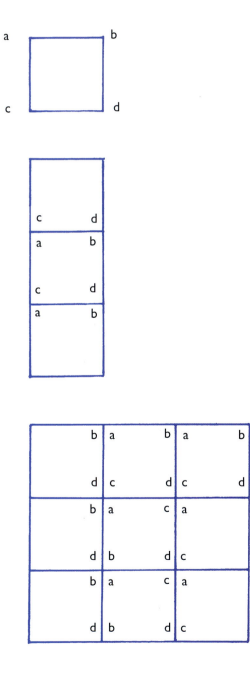

Detail of ribbon embroidery on Carolyn linen sheath dress (see opposite page)

Carolyn: Template A, pattern repeat for linen sheath dress
Enlarge at 133%

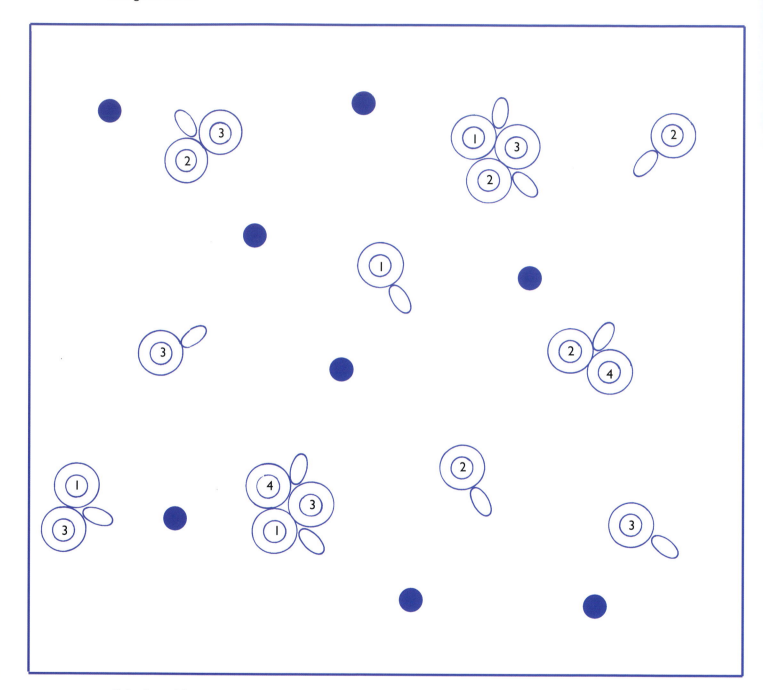

Stitch guide

all leaves—YLI #31, lazy daisy
flower #1—YLI #125, Japanese ribbon stitch
flower #2—YLI #115, Japanese ribbon stitch
flower #3—YLI #009, 4 mm, Japanese ribbon stitch
flower #4—YLI #97, Japanese ribbon stitch
dots—YLI #009, 7 mm, covered French knot

VELVETEEN PURSE
ILLUSTRATED BELOW

Materials
black velveteen purse, approx. 10 x 9 inches
(25 x 23 cm)

YLI silk ribbon (4 mm), 1 pack each:
#53, gold
#72, green
#85, purple
#93, red
template B

Carolyn design in silk ribbon turns a plain black velveteen purse into something special

Special embroidery notes

Because I used a simply made purse with a loose lining, it was easy to open up the bottom seam of that lining and reach in to access the inner side of the exterior fabric. The handling is awkward, but not difficult, especially since the purse requires so little embroidery. Look for a similarly made purse or try one of the many patterns for handbags now available. (Butterick patterns #6907 and #6371 are similar.) If you make your own bag, embroider the front piece before constructing the bag.

The Japanese ribbon stitch flowers have 16 petals in the larger bottom layer and 8 in the top.

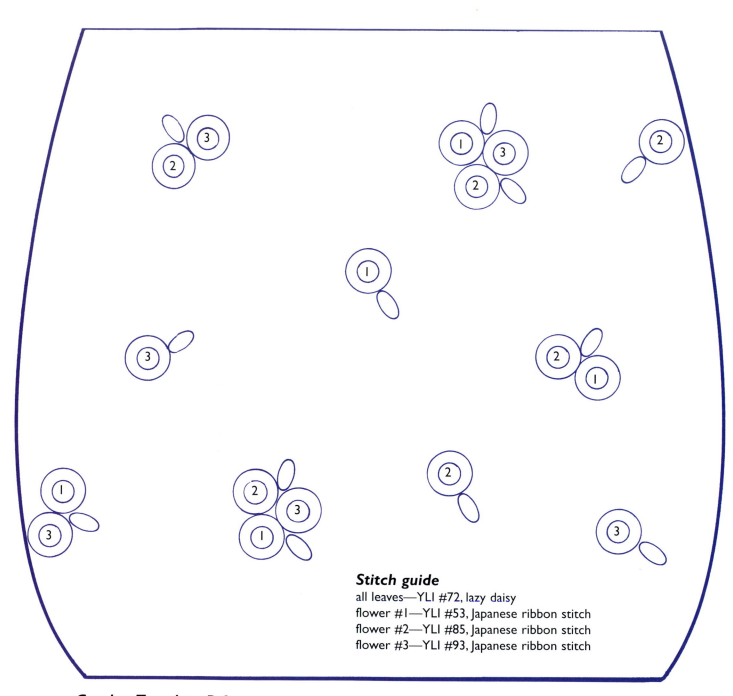

Stitch guide
all leaves—YLI #72, lazy daisy
flower #1—YLI #53, Japanese ribbon stitch
flower #2—YLI #85, Japanese ribbon stitch
flower #3—YLI #93, Japanese ribbon stitch

Carolyn: Template B for purse
Enlarge at 133%

FLEECE JACKET AND HAT
ILLUSTRATED ON PAGE 62, DETAIL BELOW

Materials
child's jacket and cap in frost blue fleece
DMC cotton floss:
> *#341, blue*
> *#703, green*
> *#962, pink*
> *#3821, yellow*
> *white*
templates C, D and E

Special embroidery notes
Follow the transfer instructions to place the design around the neck of the finished jacket and on the upturned brim of the hat. The green leaves are worked with 4 strands of floss and the blossoms with 3 strands. The bottom layer of each flower is made of 12 lazy daisy stitches, and the top layer contains 6 stitches.

Bonus ideas
Try some of these other colour options:
*Vibrant blues on black background—#11, #45,
 #81, #126, green #95*
*Bright pinks on black background—#123, #145,
 #153, #180, green #20*
*Bright pinks on white background—same as on
 black, but green #60*
*Yellows on white background—#001, #12, #13,
 #156, green #31*
*Pastels on sheer white background—#003, #83,
 #97, #100, green #31*

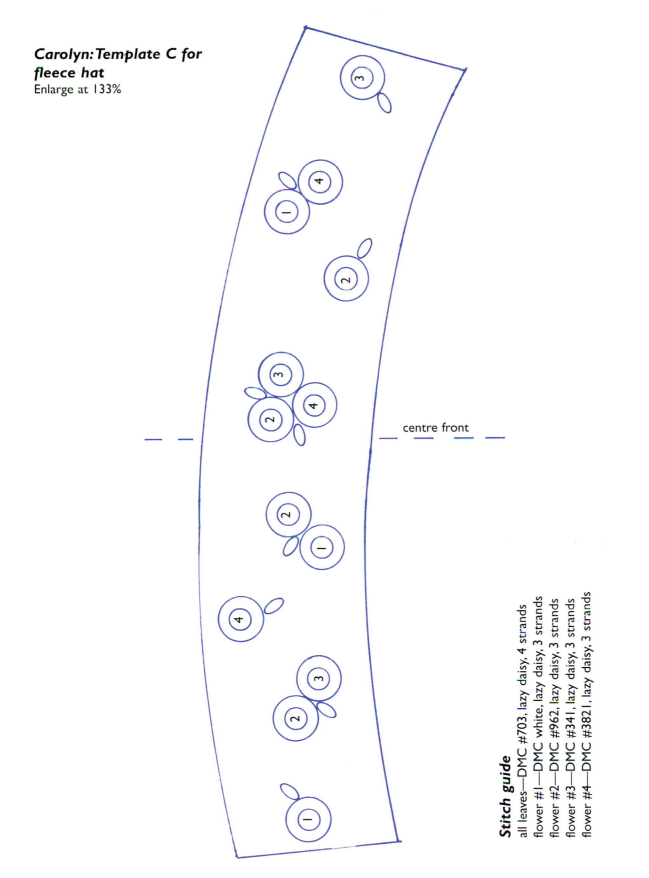

Carolyn: Template C for fleece hat
Enlarge at 133%

centre front

Stitch guide
all leaves—DMC #703, lazy daisy, 4 strands
flower #1—DMC white, lazy daisy, 3 strands
flower #2—DMC #962, lazy daisy, 3 strands
flower #3—DMC #341, lazy daisy, 3 strands
flower #4—DMC #3821, lazy daisy, 3 strands

Opposite The cheerful flowers of the Carolyn design adorn a child's fleece jacket and hat (see page 61)

Carolyn: Template D for fleece jacket
Enlarge at 133%

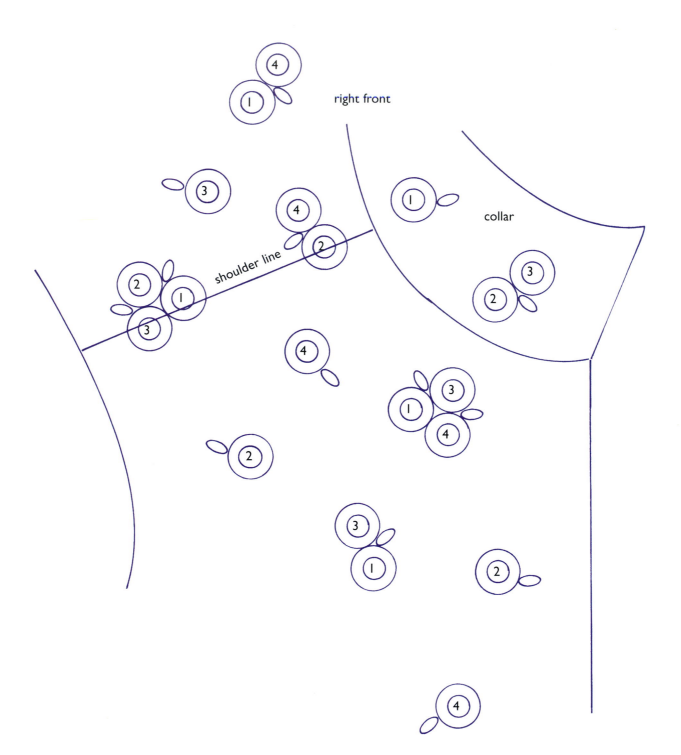

Carolyn: Template E for fleece jacket
Enlarge at 133%

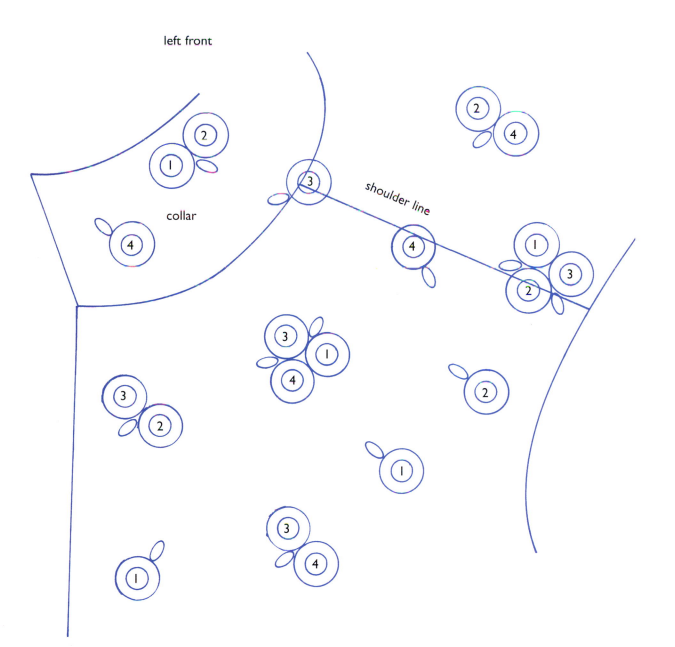

Claire

'Claire' is a simple pictorial design featuring angels and their golden musical notes. They float in pastel shades across the bodice and skirt of a child's dress and cascade in jewel tones down the slope of an elegant silk Christmas stocking. Only the most basic stitches are required to create this lovable motif.

TRANSFER

The simple lines of the angel figure makes it easy to transfer by cutting an outline and tracing around it with a fine-point chalk or soapstone pencil; the musical notes are easy to sketch freehand if you want to use them without the background lines on a dark or opaque fabric. However, the precise lines of the musical staves must be transferred more exactly if you wish to include them. If you plan to use the design as a whole, it is best to work on a more transparent fabric and trace from the template.

EMBROIDERY

Because the angels float on top of the musical background, embroider the lines of the staves first. This is done in outline stitch using 2 strands of floss.

The angels' heads are worked next in padded straight stitch, as shown in the photograph in the next column. Place three French knots in 7 mm silk ribbon #135 in the centre of the circle for the face, two in the eye area and one below, to form a triangle. Make two vertical straight stitches covering the knots, then two horizontal stitches covering the vertical ones. Finally, cover all previous stitches with two overlapping vertical

stitches placed closely side by side at the top of the head and extending to the bottom of the circle. Use the straight of your needle to smooth out any folds or wrinkles in the face, moving them toward the edges, which will be covered with stitches forming the hair.

Working with 2 strands of floss for the hair, make your first stitches at the sides of the face about mid-cheek. These will be short downward stitches covering the edges of the flesh-coloured circle you have made for the head. Make a second layer of stitches beginning a little higher up, from the temple area downward, overlapping the first set of stitches. Then, starting from the top centre of the head, make a third layer of straight

Opposite Claire girl's angel dress, embroidered in a cheerful Christmas design in cotton floss and silk ribbon on a fine cotton flannel (see page 68)

downward stitches to create bangs and cover the top of the head, overlapping the stitches already in place. You can create the semblance of parted hair by angling the bangs to one side or the other. Work until you like the look, and don't be afraid to experiment with the overall length or shape. You may want to do a practice head or two to get the feel of the technique. There is no right or wrong here. When you are satisfied with it, work the halo above the hair in stem stitch using 2 strands of floss.

Now you are ready to make the body of the angel. This is done in 7 mm ribbon with straight stitches. Make the two long vertical stitches which form the sides of the robe first, leaving the centre stitch for later. Then make the two short angled stitches for the shoulders, then the two longer angled stitches for the arms, which meet at the centre of the body. The last step is the long centre stitch that hides the ends of the arms.

The final touch to the angels is creating the wings. They get their sheer shimmer from gold spark organdie ribbon, and they are composed of a series of Japanese ribbon stitches in varying lengths as indicated by the stitch guide.

To round out the whole design, fill in the musical notes. Their stems are composed of outline stitches made with 2 strands of floss, and the bodies are padded straight stitches. Start with a single French knot done with 4 mm ribbon, and overlay it with a vertical straight stitch. Cover that with two horizontal straight stitches which are placed closely side by side and overlap each other. Note that the overall shape of the notes is closer to an oval than a circle.

GIRL'S ANGEL DRESS
ILLUSTRATED ON PAGE 67

Materials
Chery Williams 'empire waist dress' pattern,
  long sleeves
Swiss cotton flannel
¾ inch (18 mm) tatting, ¾ yd (70 cm)
½ inch (12 mm) tatting, 1 yd (1 m)
⅛ inch (3 mm) narrow elastic

DMC cotton floss:
  #415, grey
  #676, gold
  #844, soft black
  #738, honey
  #869, brown
  #977, light rust
YLI silk ribbon (4 mm):
  #53, gold
  #39, ecru spark organdie (5 mm)
YLI silk ribbon (7 mm):
  #006, pink
  #009, blue
  #31, green
  #135, flesh
  #156, yellow
templates A and B

Special embroidery notes
Seam together the skirt front and back according to pattern instructions. Template A has an 8¾ inch (22.25 cm) repeat so it will fit on the finished skirt widths after the seams have been made. You may want to trace or photocopy two or three repeats of the pattern and connect them by placing line a next to line b and taping them together. This way you won't have to reposition the template as many times when you trace the design around the entire skirt.

Use template B for the bodice motif. The centre front line will help in positioning it.

Construction notes
Omit the collar the pattern calls for and substitute a simple bias band at the neckline. Slipstitch the ¾ inch (18 mm) tatting to the band so that it lies flat on the bodice. To make the ruffled sleeve, omit the cuff pattern and elongate the sleeve pattern by 2 inches (5 cm). Finish the sleeve edge with a narrow hem or hemstitching and attach the ½ inch (12 mm) tatting to it. Measure the child's wrist and cut two pieces of elastic that length minus ½ inch (12 mm). Use a wide zigzag stitch to apply the elastic inside the sleeve, 2 inches (5 cm) from the wrist.

CHRISTMAS STOCKING
ILLUSTRATED ON PAGE 70

Materials
ecru dupion silk, 1 yd (1 m)
gold dupion silk, 1 yd (1 m)
1⅓ yds (1.25 m) flannel interfacing
3 inch (8 cm) ecru Battenburg lace, ½ yd (45 cm)
⅜ inch (8 mm) cording, 1⅔ yd (1.5 m)
medium-weight felt, 1 yd (1 m)

YLI silk ribbon (4 mm):
  #53, gold
  #65, gold spark organdie (5 mm)
YLI silk ribbon (7 mm):
  #002, red
  #20, olive green
  #45, royal blue
  #61, emerald green
  #84, violet
  #113, rose

Detail of bodice embroidery in Claire girl's dress

#117, *periwinkle*
#135, *flesh*
DMC cotton floss:
#301, *rust*
#611, *brown*
#647, *grey*
#676, *gold*
#3799, *soft black*
template C

Special embroidery notes

Draw the stocking shape with a #2 (HB) pencil. If your silk is unharmed by water, you may use a water-soluble marking pen for the embroidery design. If not, it would be best to use pencil for the entire piece. Mark the design lightly and carefully. If you get the design in the proper position you can be sure all the markings will be covered by the embroidery. Follow the embroidery instructions, and embroider the front before constructing the stocking.

Construction notes

Note that the pattern pieces for the silk exterior, the lining and the flannel interfacing are all different sizes. Cut two of each according to the template instructions.

Cut bias pieces of the gold silk to create a covering for the cording. Mark a ½ inch (12 mm) seam allowance on the right side of the embroidered stocking face, and baste the covered cord along that line, having raw edges together. Turn under ¼ inch (6 mm) on the top edge of the stocking front and back. Press and stitch.

Assemble the pieces by placing the embroidered stocking front face-to-face with the stocking back. Pin the two pieces of interfacing to the wrong sides of the first two pieces, and place the lining atop the interfacing. Stitch all six layers together along a ½ inch (12 mm) seam line, starting at one dot and stitching around the toe to the other. Make a ½ inch (12 mm) bar tack on the seam line at the appropriate marking, and clip inward from the edge to the bar tack. Trim the seam allowance and clip the curves. Turn the stocking right side out and press, gently working the clipped seam open at the bar tack. The lining and interfacing should lie flat with their edges open at the top of the stocking.

With the stocking body right side out, stitch the newly opened lining and interfacing edges along the seam line from each bar tack point up to the top of the lining. Trim the seam. Fold the top edge of the lining forward on the fold line and stitch down. Fold the lining forward once to cover the interfacing and again to cover the top edge of the embroidered front. The cuff can be held in place with a blind stitch along the bottom, tacked at the corners, or left to rest freely.

Centre the lace over the midline of the cuff and whip its top edge to the cuff's top edge, seaming the lace at the back.

Bonus idea

This design is a wonderful motif for new baby items. The repeat from the skirt of the child's dress looks great on a dust ruffle for a crib or bassinet, and the bodice design works nicely on the corner of a special blanket. Use the pastel colours from the dress project or choose your own to complement a nursery colour scheme.

Opposite Claire Christmas stocking in dupion silk and Battenburg lace, richly embroidered in silk ribbon (see page 69)

Claire: Template A for girl's angel dress bodice

bodice centre front line

See Embroidery instructions on page 68 for stitch guide

Colour guide

faces—YLI #135
#1—hair, DMC #738; robe, YLI #009
#2—hair, DMC #844; robe, YLI #006
#3—hair, DMC #977; robe, YLI #31
wings—YLI #39, ecru spark organdie
haloes—DMC #676, 2 strands
musical stave—DMC #415, 2 strands
musical notes—stems: DMC #676, 2 strands; heads, YLI #53

line b

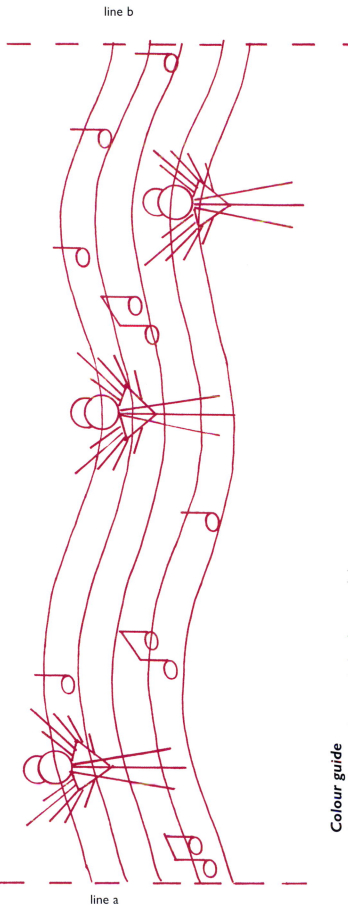

Claire: Template B for skirt repeat

line a

Colour guide

(repeat colourways in numerical order around the
circumference of the skirt, starting at any point)

angel #1—hair, DMC #738; robe, YLI #009

angel #2—hair, DMC #844; robe, YLI #006

angel #3—hair, DMC #977; robe, YLI #31

angel #4—hair, DMC #869; robe, YLI #156

(for faces, wings, haloes, musical notes and stave lines—see
template A colour guide)

Claire: Template C for stocking embroidery
Enlarge at 200%

position 3 inches (8 cm) below fold line for stocking fabric

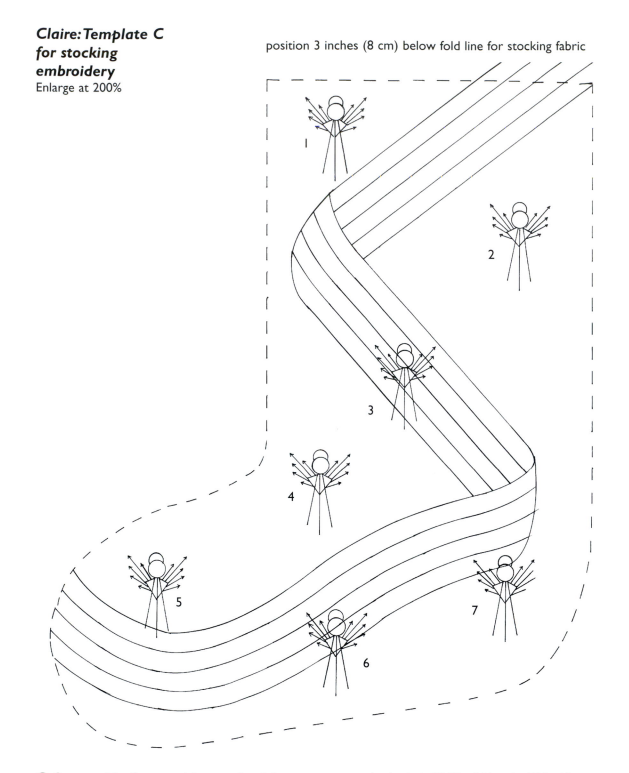

Colour guide for stocking embroidery
all faces—YLI #135
angel #1—hair, DMC #611; robe, YLI #45
angel #2—hair, DMC #3799; robe, YLI #113
angel #3—hair, DMC #301; robe, YLI #20
angel #4—hair, DMC #611; robe, YLI #117
angel #5—hair, DMC #3799; robe, YLI #002

angel #6—hair, DMC #301; robe, YLI #61
angel #7—hair, DMC #3799; robe, YLI #84
wings—YLI #65 gold spark organdie
haloes—DMC #676, 2 strands
musical stave—DMC #647, 2 strands
musical notes—stems, DMC #676, 2 strands; heads, YLI #53

Evers

Inspired by the elaborate frame of an old family mirror, 'Evers' is an unusual design with a strong architectural feel. Worked in shadow embroidery paired with silk ribbon, the balance of its rope-like texture with the elaborate scrollwork is nothing short of elegant. 'Evers' is the perfect solution when a special occasion calls for something formal for a young ring-bearer or for an older girl who disdains flowers and lace. It is especially effective for sheer home accents, such as window treatments or delicate pillows. With its emphasis on right-angled corners, the design can be worked as a square or disassembled into its decorative parts.

Detail of Evers embroidery in shadow work and silk ribbon on the bodice of the coat dress (see page 77)

Evers blouse with square collar, worked in pale yellow on a silky batiste (see opposite)

TRANSFER

Transferring this design onto your fabric will be simple because the shadow work in it requires a fairly sheer fabric. Organdie, handkerchief linen, voile or batiste (either silk, cotton or a polycotton blend) work well. Position the chosen template under your fabric and trace with a water-soluble marker on washable fabrics or lightly with a pencil on dry-clean only fabrics. Because of the size and complexity of the design, I would not recommend using a disappearing marking pen.

In a design such as this one with straight lines and right angles, while it may seem difficult to keep the lines sharp and straight, I have found that using the weave of the fabric as a guide makes it quite easy. To do this, your design must be positioned on the straight of the grain. The Chery Williams patterns used for the garments featured here have straight edges, as does the square for the pillow, so you can delineate those lines by pulling threads. When that is done and you are ready to trace the design, transfer only one of the lines of shadow work——the one which forms the square on the pillow, the longest one on the skirt and bodice designs, and the one which extends across the bottom of the collar on the blouse. (This cannot be done on the shoulders of the blouse collar or on the dress collar motifs because those pieces feature curved edges.) Measure the distances from the edges to place your tracing on the straight of the grain as closely as you can, and then embroider, placing each stitch in the same row along the weave. This may or may not exactly follow your tracing but, if you stitch carefully, your embroidered line will be correct. Wash away the marking and press to remove wrinkles. Then position the fabric again over the template, having the embroidery lined up with its corresponding template lines, and trace the entire design. Continue to use the weave as a guide as you stitch any straight line.

EMBROIDERY

All the shadow embroidery is done with a single strand of floss. Embroider the straight lines in shadow work first, then do the scrollwork in shadow embroidery as well. Fill in the lines of rope stitch done with silk ribbon next, and stitch the corner motifs last. They consist of several straight stitches in a fanlike shape with a final centre stitch laid on top, done in a Japanese ribbon stitch worked from the outside in.

BLOUSE WITH SQUARE COLLAR
ILLUSTRATED OPPOSITE

Materials
Chery Williams long and short overalls pattern,
  view 3, square-collared back-opening shirt
white silky batiste

2 yds (2.25 m) of 1 inch (2.5 cm) lace insertion
DMC cotton floss #745, pale yellow
YLI silk ribbon (2 mm) #156, pale yellow, 1 pack
templates A and B

Note The floss and ribbon colours were selected to match the fabric chosen for the accompanying knickers. You may substitute to match your choice of pants or skirt.

Special embroidery notes
To place the design properly on the collar, trace the motif onto your collar pattern, positioning it according to the template directions. Transfer the collar pattern with design onto your fabric and embroider.

Construction notes
Use view 3 on the Chery Williams pattern for your shirt or substitute any square-collared back-opening shirt you prefer. Follow pattern instructions but don't gather the lace trim. Instead, lay it flat and mitre the corners for a more tailored look. Omit the lace on the sleeves for the same reason. You will note that the lace in the photograph is actually an insertion with two straight edges; this, too, contributes to a more tailored finish.

COAT DRESS
ILLUSTRATED ON PAGE 78

Materials
Chery Williams coat dress pattern, view 3
white handkerchief linen
mini cording, 2 yds (1.85 m)
taupe bias tape, 1 pack
10–12 covered buttons, ½ inch (12 mm) diameter
DMC cotton floss #841, taupe
YLI silk ribbon (4 mm) #141, taupe, 2 packs
templates C, D and E

Special embroidery notes
Trace the skirt, bodice and collar templates onto paper. Flip them over to trace a mirror image of each to give motifs for both right and left sides.

Follow template guidelines to properly position the embroidery.

Construction notes

Using view 3 of the dress pattern, reduce the width of the collar by ¾ inch (18 mm) to avoid covering up any of the bodice embroidery. Finish the collar edge with cording covered with bias tape instead of the lace the pattern calls for. Insert covered cording into the waistline seam as well. Cover the buttons with dress fabric.

PILLOW
ILLUSTRATED ON PAGE 80

Materials

19 inch (48 cm) square pillow form
white dupion silk, ⅔ yd (60 cm)
blue dupion silk or similar fabric to match
  embroidery, ⅜ yd (35 cm)
½ inch (12 mm) cording, 1½ yds (1.75 m)
organdie, ⅔ yd (60 cm)
DMC cotton floss #800, blue
YLI silk ribbon (4 mm) #125 blue, 2 packs
templates F and G

Note Alphabet for monogram is found in 'Miriam', page 106; increase size by 175 per cent.

Special embroidery notes

Mark a 20 inch (50 cm) square on the organdie. Centre the design motif of template F inside it, trace and embroider. Organdie is abrasive and will quickly damage the silk ribbon, so work in short lengths.

Construction notes

Pull threads to mark and cut two 20 inch (50 cm) squares of white silk. Baste the embroidered organdie overlay, right side up, onto one of them. Cut the blue trim fabric into three strips measuring 4 inches (10 cm) by the width of the fabric. Using the cording, make a gathered or ruched welting for the pillow's edge (excellent instructions for this can be found in Singer's *Sewing Projects for the Home*). Pin the welting to the right side of the pillow front, raw edges together, and stitch in place with a ½ inch (12 mm) seam allowance. Sew the pillow back to the pillow front, placing right sides together. Leave a large opening along one side. Turn right side out, press, insert the pillow form, and slipstitch the open side closed.

Bonus idea

If desired, 'Evers' can be worked entirely in floss. Three slightly larger rows of satin stitch alternating with shadow work replace the four rows of alternating shadow and rope stitch, and the corner device is worked in satin stitch as well. Template G shows the motif for this alternative. Use the form shown here to redraw any of the other templates to accommodate this embroidery method. To embroider, use a single strand of floss for the shadow work and to outline and fill in the areas of satin stitch. Work the satin stitch itself in 2 strands of floss.

I think this design works best in subtle French shades. Here are a few of my favourites:

Ribbon and floss:
golden olive—YLI #56, DMC #372
terra cotta—YLI #76, DMC #3773
grey-green—YLI #74, DMC #503
grey-blue—YLI #131 or 73, DMC #927

Floss only (YLI has no matching ribbon):
dusty olive—DMC #524
grey—DMC #648
pale blue-green—DMC #928
champagne—DMC #3047

Opposite Evers coat dress embroidered in taupe floss and silk ribbon on white handkerchief linen (see page 77)

Evers design embroidered in cotton floss and silk ribbon on an organdie overlay (see page 79)

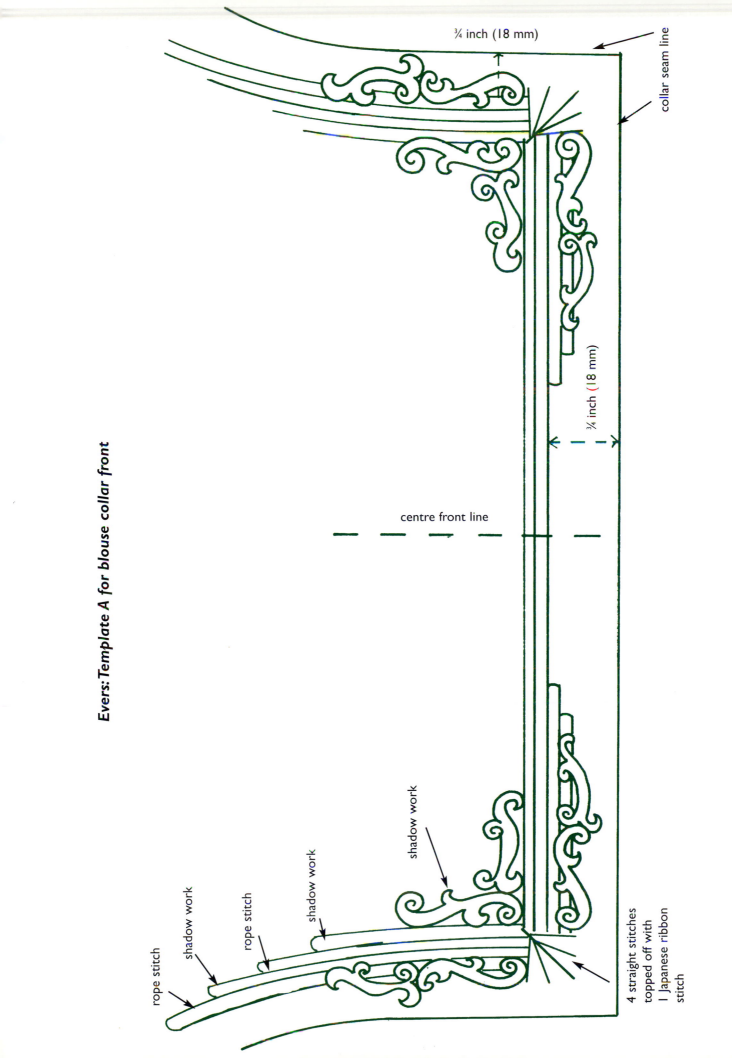

Evers: Template A for blouse collar front

¾ inch (18 mm)

collar seam line

¾ inch (18 mm)

centre front line

shadow work

shadow work

shadow work

rope stitch

rope stitch

4 straight stitches
topped off with
I Japanese ribbon
stitch

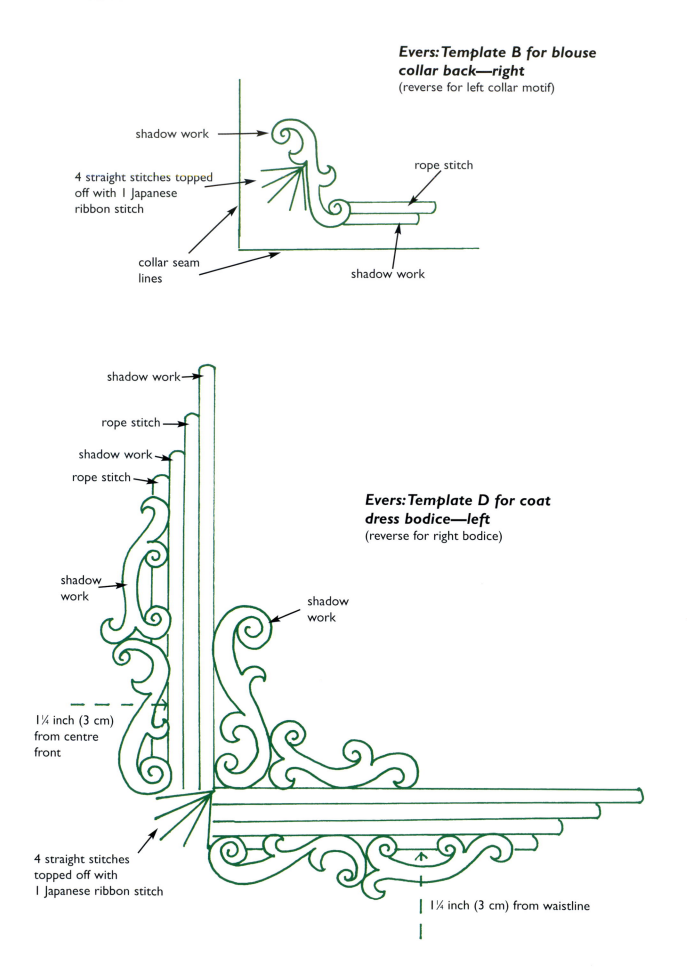

Evers: Template B for blouse collar back—right
(reverse for left collar motif)

shadow work

4 straight stitches topped off with 1 Japanese ribbon stitch

collar seam lines

rope stitch

shadow work

shadow work

rope stitch

shadow work

rope stitch

Evers: Template D for coat dress bodice—left
(reverse for right bodice)

shadow work

shadow work

1¼ inch (3 cm) from centre front

4 straight stitches topped off with 1 Japanese ribbon stitch

1¼ inch (3 cm) from waistline

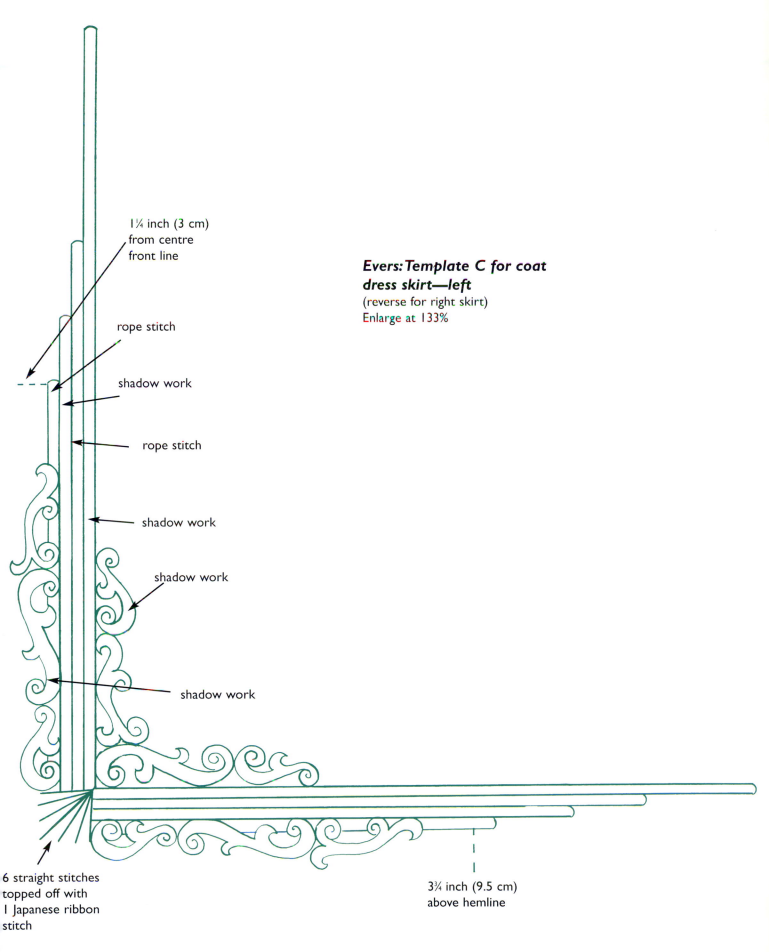

1¼ inch (3 cm) from centre front line

rope stitch

shadow work

rope stitch

shadow work

shadow work

shadow work

Evers: Template C for coat dress skirt—left
(reverse for right skirt)
Enlarge at 133%

6 straight stitches topped off with 1 Japanese ribbon stitch

3¾ inch (9.5 cm) above hemline

Evers: Template F for pillow
Enlarge at 133%

shadow work

rope stitch

shadow work

rope stitch

shadow work

6 straight stitches
topped off with
1 Japanese ribbon
stitch

Evers: Template E for coat dress collar—right
(reverse for left collar)

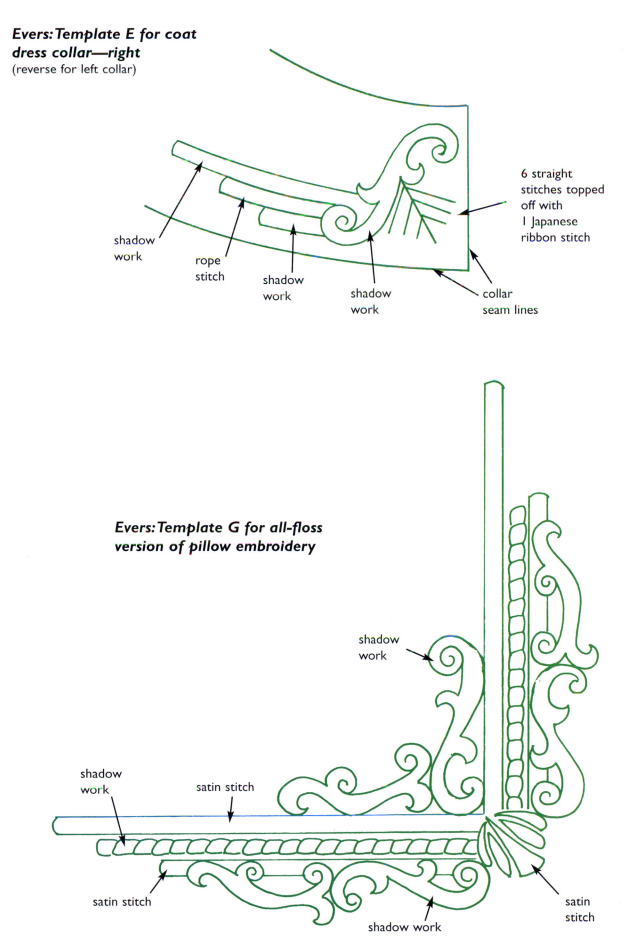

shadow work

rope stitch

shadow work

shadow work

6 straight stitches topped off with 1 Japanese ribbon stitch

collar seam lines

Evers: Template G for all-floss version of pillow embroidery

shadow work

shadow work

satin stitch

satin stitch

shadow work

satin stitch

Gerry

A simple basket of blossoms, 'Gerry' is a small design ready to provide a colourful focal point for either household linens or clothing. This chapter offers a selection of seasonal colourways for the silk ribbon embroidery option, which is featured on the bodice of a child's pinafore, as well as a subtly shaded crewel-work option shown decorating a corner of a pale silk blanket.

TRANSFER

The silk ribbon design is embroidered on a white piqué bodice and can be traced from template A with a water-soluble marker, matching up the centre line of the design with the centre front line of the bodice pattern. The woven lines making up the basket need only be indicated by dots marking the beginning and ending of each strand of ribbon.

Because the crewel design is to be worked on a heavy opaque blanket, its transfer will be a little more complicated. I recommend using a purple disappearing pen, and marking only a small section of the design at a time. This is not the most efficient method, but it will eliminate the need to wash the entire blanket when you are finished with the embroidery. Using template B, align it in the corner of your blanket as the directions indicate and mark the basket's four corners on the blanket with your pen. On a sheet of ¼ inch (5 mm) graph paper mark off a rectangle 12 squares wide and 8 squares high. Punch a small hole with a large needle or a pen at each of the intersections of all the lines in that rectangle (104 holes in all). Align the four marked corners on the blanket with the corresponding holes in your graph paper rectangle, and pin the paper to the blanket in that position. Now with your purple pen make a dot on the blanket through each hole punched in the paper. These holes will serve as guides for the split stitches used to create the woven basket. The flowers and foliage will be transferred in the same way. See the special embroidery notes for the blanket project for more detail.

EMBROIDERY

Embroider the basket first and then work the flowers following the appropriate special embroidery notes.

Opposite Gerry pinafore for a small girl embroidered in summer colours—just one of four seasonal colourways in this design (see page 88)

PINAFORE
ILLUSTRATED ON PAGE 87

Materials

*Children's Corner pattern, 'Britt', view A
  (unsmocked)
light blue micro-check gingham
white piqué, ½ yd (0.5 m)
white batiste lining, ½ yd (0.5 m)
template A*

Summer	Autumn	Winter	Spring
YLI ribbon (4 mm), 1 pack each:			
#60	#20	#154	#60
#63	#32	#131	#10
#69	#163	#007	#132
#82	#164	#141	#20
#98	#143	*Bucilla #1321 & YLI #90	#46
#147	#53	#156	#124
#168	#107	#135	#10

YLI ribbon (7 mm), 1 pack each:

#68	#113	#005	#009

DMC cotton floss:

#210	#3740	YLI ribbon #100	#772
#352	#3776	#951	#519
#605	#3722	#819	#775
#841	#830	#613	#3828

* Use Bucilla #1321 for basket; use YLI #90 for whipped stitches

Special embroidery notes

The colourway in which the pinafore has been worked is the summer version—the only one designed to match the gingham. To use one of the other seasonal colour choices, just substitute the colours given in the table.

Start the embroidery with the basket. Using the top and bottom rows of dots you marked as a guide, make 8 long vertical straight stitches from

Detail of Gerry embroidery in silk ribbon and cotton floss on the piqué yoke of the pinafore

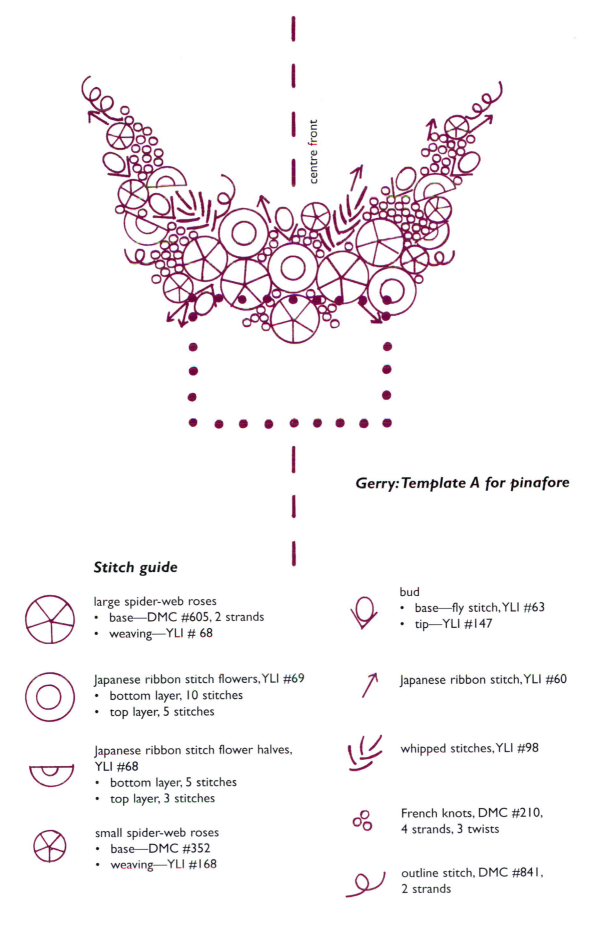

centre front

Gerry: Template A for pinafore

Stitch guide

large spider-web roses
- base—DMC #605, 2 strands
- weaving—YLI # 68

Japanese ribbon stitch flowers, YLI #69
- bottom layer, 10 stitches
- top layer, 5 stitches

Japanese ribbon stitch flower halves, YLI #68
- bottom layer, 5 stitches
- top layer, 3 stitches

small spider-web roses
- base—DMC #352
- weaving—YLI #168

bud
- base—fly stitch, YLI #63
- tip—YLI #147

Japanese ribbon stitch, YLI #60

whipped stitches, YLI #98

French knots, DMC #210, 4 strands, 3 twists

outline stitch, DMC #841, 2 strands

89

top to bottom to form the basket framework in dark blue. Tie off your ribbon at the end of each line. Then, starting and ending at the positions indicated by the two side rows of dots, make horizontal straight stitches of light blue ribbon which weave from left to right over and under successive lines of the darker ribbon, alternating the over or under position of the first stitch in each row. Once again, tie off the ribbon at the end of each line.

Follow the stitch guide for the blossoms and foliage, beginning with the large light pink roses and working your way through the flowers from largest to smallest. Save the foliage and French knots for last as they serve to fill in any empty spaces and complete the design.

Construction notes

To create the unsmocked version of this pinafore, use the front and back yoke lining pattern pieces for the actual yokes as well as their linings. Cut the front out of piqué and the back out of the gingham. Cut one of each out of batiste for the yoke linings. To showcase the embroidery better, the yoke of the US size 4 pinafore pictured was shortened by ½ inch (12 mm). This is optional and may not be

necessary in smaller pinafores. Mark and embroider the bodice front before constructing the garment. Follow pattern instructions.

BLANKET
ILLUSTRATED OPPOSITE

Materials

pale green silk fleece throw, or finished pale green
*   blanket with satin binding*
DMC #5 weight perle cotton, 1 skein each:
*   #642, taupe*
*   #746, ivory*
Appleton crewel-weight wool, 1 skein each:
*   #342, dusty olive*
*   #841, butter*
*   #951, khaki*
DMC cotton floss, 1 skein each:
*   #734, brassy green*
*   #830, sepia*
*   #832, brass*
*   #834, gold*
*   #3047, champagne*
*   #3347, medium green*
template B

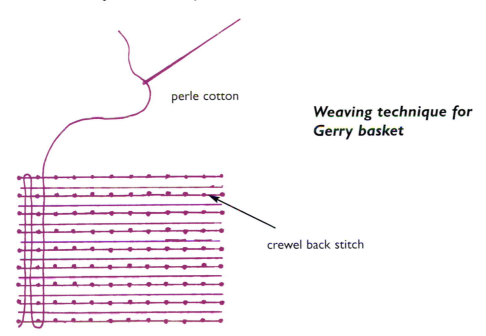

perle cotton

Weaving technique for Gerry basket

crewel back stitch

Opposite Gerry blanket embroidered in a combination of perle cotton, crewel wool and cotton floss

Gerry: Template B for blanket

centre line

4½ inches (11.5 cm) above the lowest tip of blanket fabric (not blanket binding) in any corner

Special embroidery notes

Using the dots transferred from the graph paper as a guide and working from left to right, embroider 8 horizontal lines of ¼ inch (6 mm) split stitches in the wool thread. Then embroider another horizontal row of the same size split stitches between each of the 8 finished lines. You will end up with a total of 17 horizontal lines. To complete the woven basket, thread the perle cotton in vertical lines up through the crewel stitching, starting from the left bottom corner and working up and back down, as demonstrated in the diagram below, creating 2 vertical rows of perle cotton per square of graph paper). You will have a total of 24 vertical lines.

With the basket in place, mark and embroider the blossoms. It will be best to mark and work all of one type before moving on to another. If you don't finish all of them at one sitting it will be easy to re-mark when you are ready to work again. Trace or photocopy template A onto a sheet of paper. Again using a large needle or a pen, punch holes through the paper to indicate the centre and outer circumference of each flower. Positioning the template appropriately over the embroidered basket, and using a disappearing pen, mark the position of the blossoms you plan to work. When you finish all of one type, mark another and embroider it. Continue until all blossoms are completed. As a general rule, you should start with the largest and most central flowers, in this case the lazy daisy blossoms in perle cotton. They are composed of two layers of lazy daisy stitches which overlap. Work the bottom layer first, with stitches starting on the small circle and reaching to the outer circle. The second layer's stitches begin from the centre and reach to just past the base of the stitches in the bottom ring. When those blooms are completed, work your way down the scale, saving the foliage and the French knots for last because they function as fill-ins for the remaining empty space.

Stitch guide for template B

lazy daisy blooms—DMC perle #746, 1 strand
whole blooms—bottom ring, 10 stitches; top ring, 5 stitches
half blooms—bottom, 5 stitches; top, 3 stitches

bullion roses
all centres—DMC #734, 3 strands
- 1 large—2 bullions, 8 wraps each; 3 bullions, 16 wraps each
- 2 small—2 bullions, 6 wraps each; 2 bullions, 13 wraps each
outer petals—DMC #3047, 3 strands
- large and small—8 bullions, 18 wraps each

spider-web roses
- base—Appleton crewel wool #841, 1 strand
- weaving—Appleton crewel wool #841, 2 strands

buds
- 3 feather stitches—DMC #832 floss, 4 strands
- 3 straight stitches— DMC #746 perle, 1 strand

outline stitch, DMC #830, 2 strands

3 long straight stitches, DMC #3347, 6 strands

French knots, DMC #834, 4 strands, 3 twists

outline stitch, Appleton crewel wool #342, 1 strand

Lauren

This design varies somewhat from the others in that it involves a story. When Lauren announced her intention to marry, her creative mother Virginia presented her with a beautiful family heirloom—a Brussels lace tablecloth inherited from the bride's great-grandmother—which Virginia had the imagination to envision as a bridal veil. Her vision became reality, and Lauren's wedding gown and its cathedral-length train were designed to complement it.

Detail of the wedding veil of heirloom Brussels lace which inspired the Lauren embroidery designs

Lauren ring-bearer's pillow with the initials of the bride and groom embroidered in ecru cotton floss on white Swiss batiste

I became involved in my friend's project when she asked me to create embroidery designs for two ring-bearer's pillows based on the lace configurations in the veil. She requested that the pillows be different but related. Focusing on a circle of interlocking ovals with a large petalled flower at its base, which recurred throughout the lace, I worked up a common motif for them both. For one pillow I embroidered two small versions of that circle surrounding the bride and groom's initials, and within their intersection I placed the date of the wedding. The second design featured a larger-scale copy of the same circle surrounding the bride's new, married initials. The embroidery became the focal points of two exquisite small pillows which were carried in the wedding ceremony and eventually became keepsakes.

This makes a sweet story in itself, but there is more. When Lauren was expecting her first child, Virginia opened her treasure trove, a lifetime accumulation of wonderful laces and ideas, to create a one-of-a-kind baptismal gown. Wanting to incorporate the wedding embroidery motif in this gown, she asked me to create another related design for the skirt's fancy band and bodice that would provide spaces for the initials and baptismal dates of the first grandchild and all future babies who would wear it. That design and the designs for the pillows are offered here. Feel free to borrow them, or perhaps you will be inspired by Lauren's story to search through your own heirlooms to create an embroidery motif for the significant days of your family's history.

Detail of fancy band in skirt of heirloom baptismal gown

TRANSFER

All designs were transferred by tracing with a water-soluble marking pen. Because of the small scale of some of the elements, I used a fine-tip marker. Consult the alphabets in 'Aislinn' (page 42) and 'Miriam' (page 106) for the monograms, or use your favourite. To lengthen the repeat motif for the fancy band on the christening dress, photocopy or trace several copies of template C and tape them together, lining up line a with line b.

Detail of embroidered monogram on the bodice of the baptismal gown

Lauren ring-bearer's pillow embroidered with the bride's married initials in ecru cotton floss on Swiss batiste

EMBROIDERY

Use 2 strands of ecru floss on the large monogram design for the letters and the base motif of blossom, branches and leaves. Use 1 strand of the same colour for the outline and seed stitches forming the circle in that design and for all the embroidery in the double monogram design, the fancy band and dress bodice designs.

Follow the stitch guides.

Construction notes

To respect Virginia and Lauren's desire to have the dress and pillows remain unique to their family, and because some of the materials cannot be duplicated, specific construction notes are not included in this chapter. You are invited to study the photographs for inspiration, however, and create your own special pieces. You will find clear directions for many similar gowns and pillows in *French Hand Sewing for Infants* by Sarah Howard Stone (see Resources, page 151).

HEIRLOOM EMBROIDERED PILLOWS AND DRESS

Materials

two 11 x 7 inch (28 x 18 cm) pillow forms
white Swiss batiste
white entredeux
coordinated lace insertion and edging in ecru
DMC cotton floss, ecru
templates A, B, C, D and E

**Lauren: Template A
for pillow I**

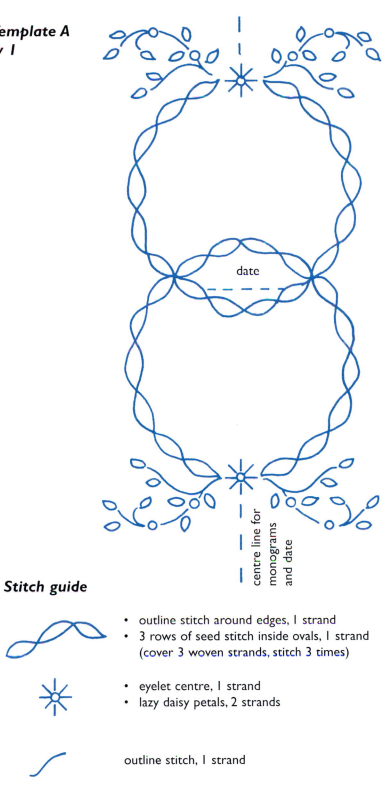

date

centre line for
monograms
and date

Stitch guide

- outline stitch around edges, I strand
- 3 rows of seed stitch inside ovals, I strand
  (cover 3 woven strands, stitch 3 times)

- eyelet centre, I strand
- lazy daisy petals, 2 strands

outline stitch, I strand

satin stitch, I strand

eyelet, I strand

Opposite Lauren baptismal gown, embroidered in a design derived from the embroidery on the wedding veil
and ring-bearers' pillows

99

Lauren: Template B for pillow 2

centre line for monogram

Stitch guide
(all stitches DMC ecru floss)

- outline stitch around edges, 2 strands
- 5–6 rows of seed stitch inside ovals, 1 strand (cover 5 woven strands, stitch 3 times)

satin stitch
- outline and fill, 1 strand
- satin work, 2 strands

- eyelet centre, 1 strand
- lazy daisy petals, 2 strands

outline stitch, 2 strands

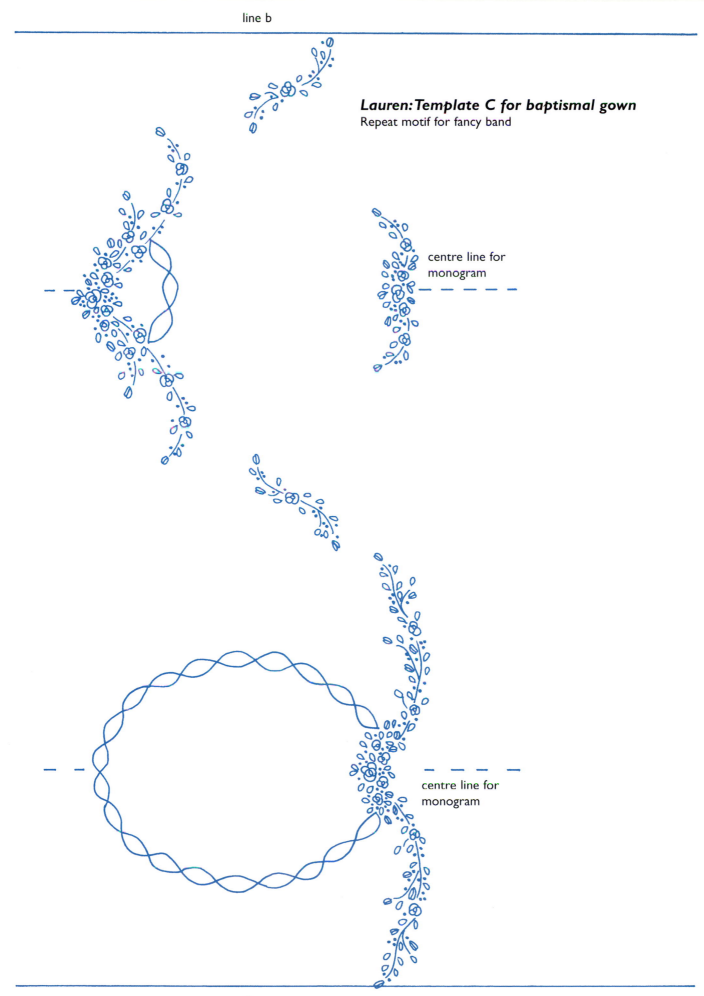

Lauren: Template C for baptismal gown
Repeat motif for fancy band

centre line for
monogram

centre line for
monogram

Stitch guide for templates C and D
(all stitches 1 strand of DMC ecru floss)

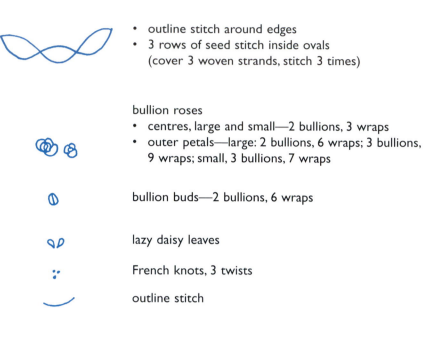

- outline stitch around edges
- 3 rows of seed stitch inside ovals
  (cover 3 woven strands, stitch 3 times)

bullion roses
- centres, large and small—2 bullions, 3 wraps
- outer petals—large: 2 bullions, 6 wraps; 3 bullions, 9 wraps; small, 3 bullions, 7 wraps

bullion buds—2 bullions, 6 wraps

lazy daisy leaves

French knots, 3 twists

outline stitch

Lauren: Template D for baptismal gown

bodice motif for gown

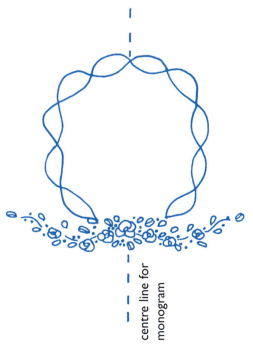

centre line for monogram

Stately formal letters, entwined with silk trumpets—what could be more elegant than the 'Miriam' alphabet? You will find lots of ways to use this unusual set of letters, so it is accompanied by a diverse set of accents, allowing you to create monograms that fit your individual style. The projects here, worked in silk ribbon and/or cotton floss, illustrate only a fraction of the possibilities for this design. They include a hand towel with a cool, classic oval motif; a framed monogram with a Victorian touch; a young boy's formal linen shirt accented with an arch borrowed from a stained glass window; and a richly tasselled pillow in which the bold letters stand on their own. You'll also recognise the letter style as that on the front of the delicate silk pillow in 'Evers'. Let your imagination have free rein as you explore your own ideas inspired by these designs.

TRANSFER

All four projects were traced from their respective templates using a water-soluble marker. Choose the letters you need from the alphabet in template A. If your project is one with a larger-sized centre letter (which is usually that of the family name), use a photocopier to increase its size. Consult 'Aislinn' (page 36) for instructions on the proper placement and spacing of a monogram. When you have your letters correctly positioned, trace any accompanying motif around them, aligning the monogram's centre line with that of the surrounding design.

EMBROIDERY

In the first three projects presented here, the letters are worked in satin stitch with 2 strands of floss for a rich, heavy look. In an odd coincidence, the colour schemes chosen for all three presented challenges which were solved in each case by combining different threads in the needle. Whether you choose to use the colours illustrated here or not, this is a useful technique which will serve you well in future projects.

After I fell in love with the fabulous tasselled trim which finishes the edge of the tiny pillow in the first project, I discovered that DMC did not have a rose floss in a shade which matched to my satisfaction. Realising that I would be using a double strand of thread in my needle, I decided to create my own shade by combining two of the colours I was trying to choose between. When they are used together, you can see a definite texture caused by the difference in colour, but this is a plus in this case because it echoes the multitude of colours in the trim.

A similar situation arose when I tried to find a floss to match the YLI ribbon I wanted to use for

Miriam tasselled pillow in heavy linen embroidered in silk ribbon and cotton floss (see opposite page)

the trumpets around the monogram in the Victorian frame and on the hand towel. The looping coils of that motif are embroidered with floss to look as if they form the tapering end of the trumpet flare which is done in ribbon; it is important for the illusion that the ribbon and the floss be as close as possible in colour. Again, combining two colours gave me what I needed. In these two cases the colours were so pale that it was impossible to distinguish them, and they just blended to create a new shade. Of course this trick only works if you are using two or more

strands of floss in your needle, but it can be quite useful.

The flared motif decorating the letters looks a bit unusual, but is just a simple outline stitch. The delicate ends, indicated by a single line, are done in 2 strands of floss which, at points hidden behind the legs of the letter they decorate, gives way to matching ribbon, as shown in the diagram on page 111. When making the outline stitches with the wide ribbon, keep your stitches loose and puffy, follow the stitch guide, and you will be pleased with your results. On a sheer fabric, this part of the design could be done in a shadow stitch. Explore the options of combining shadow work, satin stitch, silk ribbon and crewel work, and you will find lots of ways to customise this design for your own look, working with the stitches you do best.

TASSELLED PILLOW
ILLUSTRATED OPPOSITE

Materials
heavy ecru linen, ⅓ yd (30 cm)
1½ yds (1.4 m) tasselled trim
polyester batting
YLI silk ribbon (7 mm):
  #35, dull gold
DMC cotton floss:
  #223, mauve rose
  #833, bright gold
  #3722, deep rose
templates A and B
approximate measurements 7 x 10 inches
  (18.75 x 25 cm)

Special embroidery notes
Although intended to be a tiny lady's pillow, the exact dimensions for this project were determined by the 1¼ inch (3 cm) repeat in the tasselled trim. I wanted to highlight its elaborate design and place the trim flat on the pillow face, with the corners mitred for a neat finish. Working with the length of the repeat allowed me to ensure that all four corners would be identical. To find the repeat in your trim, locate two consecutive places in the design which are identical, and measure the distance between them. Your pillow's finished dimensions, both length and width, should be in multiples of that number.

When you have determined the finished size of your pillow, add ½ inch (12 mm) to both measurements to allow yourself a ¼ inch (6 mm) seam allowance all the way around. Pull threads to mark those dimensions on your fabric. Find the centre of the front and mark your monogram. For this monogram, the smaller letters were enlarged by 115 per cent, the larger one by 135 per cent.

Embroider the letters first in satin stitch. Outline and fill with a single strand of either of the two colours chosen. Do the satin stitch itself with 2 strands of floss, threading your needle with 1 strand of each shade of rose. Outline stitch around each finished letter with 1 strand of the gold floss. Create the trumpets with two curves worked in outline stitch done with the 7 mm ribbon, as the stitch guide indicates. Use 2 strands of gold floss in outline stitch to complete the tapering ends.

Construction notes
After the embroidery is completed, pin the trim in place on the pillow face, mitring the corners. Stitch in place. Cut out the pillow front and back and pin together with right sides facing, keeping the fringe out of the stitch path. Stitch them together all the way around except for an opening along one long side. Turn right side out, fill with batting and slipstitch the opening closed.

FRAMED MONOGRAM
ILLUSTRATED ON PAGE 107

Materials
cream linen, ⅓ yd (30 cm)
YLI silk ribbon (4 mm):
  #76, terra cotta
  #178, mulberry
YLI silk ribbon (7 mm):
  #65, pale mauve
DMC cotton floss:
  #948, pale blush
  #950, flesh
  #3042, mulberry
  #3046, medium gold
  #3053, green
  #3773, terra cotta
  #3774, pale peach
  #3782, beige
templates A and C
purchased frame

Miriam: Template A

Miriam framed monogram, richly embroidered in silk ribbon and cotton floss on ecru linen

Special embroidery notes

Centre your design in the middle of your fabric; this will allow plenty of room for whatever type of framing you choose to use. The motif was designed to suit an oval outline; if an oval frame is hard to find, consider an oval-shaped matting inside a rectangular frame.

Embroider the central letter first, then the trumpet shapes. Start at the tapered end of the trumpet with 2 strands of floss, making an outline stitch. Switch to ribbon where the trumpet widens, and back to floss where it tapers again. Moving on to the flowers, start with the largest ones first, the spider-web roses. The gathered roses should be embroidered next, then the bullion roses and leaves. Fill in the French knots and the curlicues on the top motif last.

Construction notes

Starch and press your fabric, avoiding the ribbon embroidery. A quilter's mini-iron is a wonderful aid in doing this. Have your finished work framed by a framer with experience in stretching and framing needlework, taking care to emphasise that ribbon embroidery must not be flattened.

HAND TOWEL
ILLUSTRATED OPPOSITE

Materials
lace-trimmed linen hand towel
YLI silk ribbon (2 and 7 mm):
   #001, white
DMC cotton floss:
   #822, silvered khaki
   white
   ecru
templates A and D

Special embroidery notes

This design requires both 2 and 7 mm widths of the same colour ribbon. As not all of YLI's colours come in both widths, if you want to use a different colour scheme from the neutral one shown here, be sure that both widths are available before you start.

YLI makes two shades of white ribbon—#001 is slightly creamy, #003 is a purer white. Since I chose to use #001, I needed a white floss with a creamy cast to it. To get this I threaded 1 strand each of DMC's white and ecru into my needle. If you choose to use the #003 ribbon, you need only use white floss.

The monogram letter was enlarged by 135 per cent. Embroider it first, and then the frame around it. The 2 mm ribbon is used to make the texture pattern within the oval framework, simply a series of small straight stitches. Do the trumpet motif last. Your outline stitches will begin with 2 strands of floss, change

to the 7 mm ribbon and then back to floss again. As a final touch, 4 strands of the embroidery floss used for the letter were woven through the heading of the wide lace edging. Knots securing each end were hidden at the back of the towel.

BOY'S LINEN SUIT
ILLUSTRATED ON PAGE 110

Materials
Chery Williams 'button-on suits' pattern, short-
   sleeved shirt (unsmocked) and boy's long pants
   (shortened to above-knee length)
dusty olive green heavy linen
ecru handkerchief linen
DMC cotton floss:
   #524, dusty green
   #3013, brass
1¼ yds (1.15 m) ecru heirloom tatting
templates A and E

Special embroidery notes

Centre the letter of your choice in its original size inside the round motif of template E on tracing or graph paper. Transfer to the shirt front, positioning the design on the garment's centre front line. Trace the sleeve pattern piece onto your fabric, then flip it over and trace its mirror image for the second sleeve. Position the sleeve embroidery template on each sleeve according to the instructions, and trace. The sleeves should be worked before the shirt is constructed, but the shirt front can be done before or after construction. Follow the stitch guide. All the embroidery is done with a single strand of floss.

Construction notes

Follow the pattern instructions, shortening the pleated pants to the desired length. The buttons on the waistband are optional; they are usually omitted on pants for older boys. Attach tatting to the shirt collar and cuffs.

Opposite Miriam hand towel, embroidered in subtle colours

Embroidering the trumpet

The arrows indicate the direction of the stitches in the trumpet. The outline stitch done with silk ribbon begins on the lower left side of the letter and follows the path of the lower arrow. A second line of outline stitches begins where the upper arrow starts and ends at the top right side of the letter. The single curling lines indicate where the outline stitch is worked in floss.

Miriam: Template B for tasselled pillow

Placement guide for monogram

top line for first and
middle name initials

centre line

base line for first and middle
name initials

Colour guide

letters—DMC #223 and #3722

trumpets
• flares—YLI #35
• coiled ends—DMC #833, 2 strands

See special embroidery notes on page 105 for stitch guide

Opposite Boy's green linen suit top embroidered with a monogram from the Miriam alphabet; elements of the surrounding 'frame' are repeated on collar and sleeves

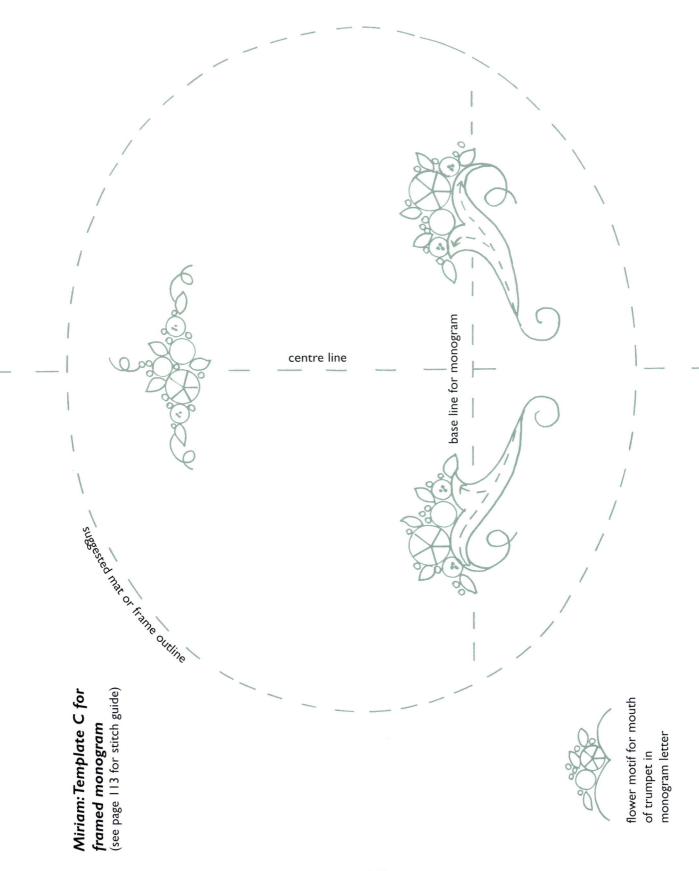

centre line

base line for monogram

suggested mat or frame outline

Miriam: Template C for framed monogram (see page 113 for stitch guide)

flower motif for mouth of trumpet in monogram letter

Miriam: Template D for hand towel

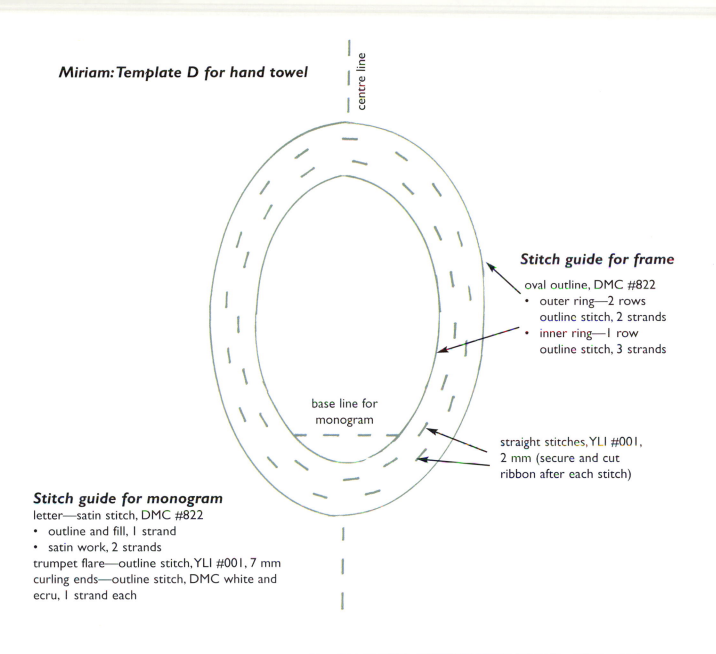

centre line

Stitch guide for frame

oval outline, DMC #822
*   outer ring—2 rows
    outline stitch, 2 strands
*   inner ring—1 row
    outline stitch, 3 strands

base line for
monogram

straight stitches, YLI #001,
2 mm (secure and cut
ribbon after each stitch)

Stitch guide for monogram

letter—satin stitch, DMC #822
*   outline and fill, 1 strand
*   satin work, 2 strands
trumpet flare—outline stitch, YLI #001, 7 mm
curling ends—outline stitch, DMC white and
ecru, 1 strand each

Stitch guide for framed monogram (template C on page 112)

cornucopia trumpets
*   flares—outline stitch, YLI #65
*   curled ends—outline stitch, DMC #948 and #3774, 1 strand each

spider-web rose
*   base—DMC #3773, 2 strands
*   weaving—YLI #76

satin stitch leaves, DMC #3053,
1 strand

gathered rose—YLI #178, gathered
with 1 strand DMC #3042

French knots, DMC #3782, 3 strands,
2 twists

bullion rose
*   centre—3 French knots, DMC #3046,
    1 strand, 2 twists
*   bullions, all DMC #950, 1 strand—
    3 bullions, 7 wraps; 4 bullions, 14 wraps

outline stitch vines, DMC #3053,
1 strand

113

Miriam: Template E for boy's suit

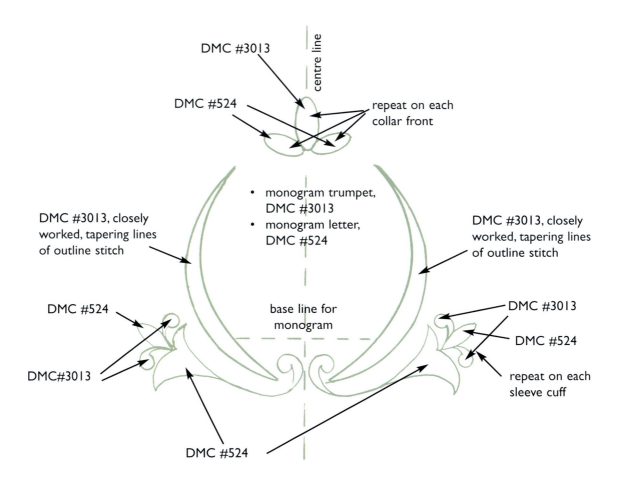

DMC #3013

centre line

DMC #524

repeat on each collar front

- monogram trumpet, DMC #3013
- monogram letter, DMC #524

DMC #3013, closely worked, tapering lines of outline stitch

DMC #3013, closely worked, tapering lines of outline stitch

base line for monogram

DMC #524

DMC #3013

DMC#3013

DMC #524

repeat on each sleeve cuff

DMC #524

all embroidery—satin stitch, 1 strand of floss except where noted

Paige

'Paige' is a richly textured border which features a central lattice design flanked on either side with flowers and foliage. It is a real attention-stealer, whether it is used in its silk-ribbon, crewelwork or traditional floss-embroidered version. A colourful way to emphasise the lines of a garment, it adds motion and excitement to any project.

TRANSFER

There are three different templates for 'Paige', one for each form of embroidery in which it has been interpreted. The silk-ribbon version appears on an older child's formal dress of dupion silk, the crewel design is on a wool challis shawl, and the cotton floss was used on a child's organdie dress. All three were traced from the appropriate template onto the fabric with a removable water-based marking pen. Because of the precision of the trellis lines at the centre of the design, as well as the complexity of the floral pattern, this design should be worked on a fabric transparent enough to allow clear tracing. Also make sure that whatever fabric you choose can withstand the application of the water necessary to remove your markings. The removal of pen marks on the wool and the silk used for the featured items could be accomplished by simply spraying a light mist of water onto the finished needlework. The organdie was immersed in water. Test whatever fabrics you plan to use. Marking lightly with pencil is an option for dry-clean only fabrics, but care should be taken that all the markings are covered by the embroidery as they are difficult to remove.

All three designs are repeat patterns, and the template for each is a short section meant to be extended. To do this, photocopy or trace several copies of the template and place your copies end-to-end with line a abutting line b. Use the extensions of the latticework as an aid in aligning the sections.

EMBROIDERY

The differences between the three forms of embroidery in which this pattern was worked required some significant changes in the design from one interpretation to the next, thus specific embroidery instructions are included in the directions for each project. One point, however, is the same for all three interpretations—-the floral design should always be worked first, then the latticework. This cuts down on the abrasion that would occur if you were moving your embroidery hoop back and forth across the finished lattice stitches.

SQUARE-NECKED SILK DRESS
ILLUSTRATED OPPOSITE

Materials
honeydew (pale green) dupion silk
Simplicity pattern #7923, view C
DMC cotton floss, 1 skein each:
   #739, beige
   #3713, pink
YLI silk ribbon:
   #34, beige (4 mm and 7 mm)
   #155, pale green (4 mm)
   #157, pink (4 mm)
ivory pearls, 3 mm
templates A and B

Note This design takes lots of ribbon and pearls. To estimate the amounts you require, allow the following for each 18 inches (45 cm) of the design: #34 (4 mm)—3 yds (2.5 m); #34 (7 mm)—8⅓ yds (7.5 m); #155—7¾ yds (7.2 m); #157—9¾ yds (9 m); 200 pearls.

Special embroidery notes
Template A is a short section of the design you will trace onto the sleeves, waistband and neckline of your dress. It can be lengthened by repeating it as many times as needed to cover the desired area. Trace the garment-pattern pieces for the sleeve and waistband onto your fabric, noting that you will need to widen the waistband to accommodate the width of the design. Zigzag the raw edges of any pieces you work with because the silk frays easily. Mark and embroider the border motif; remove your markings and assemble the pieces as you construct the dress.

The border around the square neckline will have to make four right-angle turns, and the exact design will vary depending on the size of the garment. Template B is the pattern for the US size 14 dress featured here and can be used as a guide for drawing the neckline motif for your dress. Pin the bodice pattern pieces together at the shoulder seams to form the square neckline. Trace the entire neckline onto a sheet of tracing paper. Photocopy or trace 5 copies of template A. Cut and position them under your tracing until they fit together as on template B. To accommodate the shoulder-line curve, add or subtract flowers and foliage. Remember to avoid the seam allowance at the inside neckline edge. Trace your neckline motif onto the tracing paper.

Assemble the bodice of the dress and attach the neck facings (the facings are important: they lend stability to the neckline and keep it from stretching out of shape during all the handling in the embroidery process). Don't put in the zipper, make the underarm side seams, or slipstitch the linings in place. Zigzag all raw edges to prevent fraying, and press open the shoulder seams. Lay the bodice out flat and trace the embroidery pattern onto it. You can now embroider the entire design in place.

For all areas to be embroidered, begin with the floral design on the edges of the motif, then work the trellis, and save the application of the pearls until last. Follow the stitch guide for the flowers and foliage.

For the latticework, cut short lengths of ribbon and make one long straight stitch for each line, tying off each piece as you make the stitch. Work all the lines in one direction first, alternating the beige, pink, and green colours. Then work the lines slanting in the opposite direction, weaving each ribbon alternately over and under the lines previously stitched. When all the latticework is in place, use sewing thread, not beading thread (beading thread is wiry and may be irritating to a child's skin), to stitch a pearl over each intersection of ribbon. You may move from pearl to pearl without cutting your thread, but be sure to tie a knot under each one at the back of the work to secure them. Using the same method, apply pearls where indicated among the flowers.

Opposite Paige square-necked girl's dress in honeydew-coloured dupion silk

Construction notes

Follow the pattern instructions, omitting the rosettes on the waistband. For older girls the sash may be shortened at the back by using a simple button closure with two small covered buttons instead of a bow. Shorten the sleeves to three-quarter length.

Bonus colourway for square-necked silk dress

Try these creamy pastels on white.
DMC cotton floss:
  for #739, substitute #819, pale pink
  for #3713, substitute #712, butter
YLI silk ribbon:
  for #34 (4 and 7 mm), substitute #005,
  pale pink
  keep #155, pale green
  for #157, substitute #12, butter
  for ivory 3 mm pearls, substitute white

FRINGED SHAWL
ILLUSTRATED OPPOSITE

Materials

McCall's pattern #9661, view 1
cream wool challis
matching silk or polyester lining
Appleton crewel-weight wool, 1 skein each:
  #203, medium purple
  #331, gold
  #353, medium green
  #354, dark green
  #461, light periwinkle
  #541, light green
  #891, lavender
  #892, medium periwinkle
  #893, dark periwinkle
  #951, tan
template C

Special embroidery notes

Pull threads to delineate the dimensions of the pattern pieces for your shawl. This will be more accurate than pinning the pattern to the fabric and will ensure that your pieces are aligned with the grain of the fabric. Elongate template C to fit the width of your pattern piece. Place it under the fabric and trace onto each end of the shawl, stopping at the ½ inch (12 mm) seam allowance at each side.

Start your embroidery with the large lazy daisy blooms, positioning the 12 decorative lazy daisy stitches as you would the hours on a clock face. I find it easiest to make the stitches at the 12 and the 6, the 3 and the 9 first; then I add the 2 stitches between each of them. The daisy's centre is filled in with 6 French knots.

Make the spider-web roses next. These are worked just as they are in ribbon embroidery. Use #461 for the framework, then thread #461 and #893 into the needle together to weave around the frame. For this purpose you may want to use a larger needle with a blunter tip, perhaps a #20 tapestry, to avoid snagging either the fabric or the other stitches as you work.

The leaves are done in outline and straight stitches and the small blossoms in lazy daisy and straight stitches. The clusters of berries have a fly-stitch base in green, and the berries themselves are worked in seed stitch, repeating the stitch 3 times over 3 woven threads in the same spot to build up a rounded shape.

The lines of the lattice are worked in a split stitch using relatively long stitches, ¼–⅜ inch (6–8 mm). At the intersection of the latticework, the colourful accents are made with 3 side-by-side vertical straight stitches in either periwinkle or green, alternating along each row.

Construction notes

Follow the pattern directions for a shawl with or without a seam, depending on the width of your fabric. You may add a purchased fringe or, as was done here, create fringe from your own fabric. To

Paige fringed shawl embroidered in crewel-weight wool

do this cut 6 strips of fabric 18 inches wide by 4½ inches long (45 x 11.5 cm), using the pulled-thread method to ensure that the strips are straight on the grain of the fabric. Mark a ½ inch (12 mm) seam line along one 18 inch (45 cm) side of each strip. Apply a thin line of fray stopper along this marking. After it has dried completely, pin the strips together in two sets of 3 and, using a very small zigzag stitch, sew each set together along that seam line. Pin one stitched set to each end of the shawl following the directions for attaching fringe in pattern view H. Stitch in place. Turn the shawl right side out and press the seam. Gently pull the horizontal threads, one by one, out of the fabric strips to create the fringe.

ORGANDIE PARTY DRESS
ILLUSTRATED OPPOSITE

Materials

Vogue pattern #9416, view C

white Swiss organdie; add ½ yd (0.5 m) for skirt alteration

white silky batiste; add ½ yd (0.5 m) for skirt alteration

DMC cotton floss, 1 skein each:
  #445, lemon yellow
  #725, bright gold
  #726, yellow
  #745, pale yellow
  #3821, deep gold
  white
DMC cotton floss, 2 skeins each:
  #368, green
  #471, olive green
  #704, spring green
template D

Special embroidery notes

The garment pattern for the skirt of this dress is cut on a slant, which would make it difficult for the embroidery to meet neatly at the side seams, and is not as full as in a traditionally cut dress. To correct this, allow one width of your fabric (fine organdie is usually 45 inches or 115 cm wide) for the skirt front and another for the back. Split the skirt back down the middle and seam it together to accommodate the back opening. In order to match up the design's 2 inch (5 cm) repeat neatly around the skirt, you will need to adjust the seam allowances so that the finished skirt circumference ends up an even number (in inches) or a number divisible by 5 (in metric measurements).

Assemble the skirt and hem it before you mark the embroidery design on it. Template D is a 6 inch (15 cm) segment of the repeat design. You may want to make a larger template by tracing or photocopying template D several times and taping those copies together, placing line a next to line b. Position the bottom of the design at the top of the hem and move it around the skirt as you trace a continuous circle.

Draw the Vogue bodice front #10 and bodice back #12 onto the organdie, making sure you place #10 on the fold of the fabric. Mark the ⅝ inch (15 mm) seam allowance line at the top of those pieces. Position the template used for the skirt just below that line and trace onto the fabric. Avoid the seam allowances at the underarm seams. Your embroidery will not match up perfectly there, but will not be noticeable.

The latticework in this interpretation is done in a fine chain stitch, using a single strand of floss. The stitches are ⅛ inch (3 mm) long, and consistency in size is important to the appearance of your work. If this is a problem for you, when you mark the latticework onto your fabric use a ruler and mark a series of dots ⅛ inch (3 mm) apart instead of drawing straight lines. This will give you a guide for the length of your stitches.

Construction notes

The lining and the binding at the neckline and armholes are cut from the silky batiste. Follow pattern instructions for the construction of the rest of the dress, omitting the shoulder bows.

Opposite Paige organdie party dress, richly embroidered in delicate colours in cotton floss

Detail of embroidery on Paige organdie party dress

Paige: Template A for square-necked silk dress
pattern repeat

line a

line b

Stitch guide

latticework
- 1 straight stitch for each line; alternate between YLI #34, #155 and #157 (all 4 mm)
- secure each intersection with 1 pearl

spider-web rose
- base—DMC #739, 2 strands
- weaving—YLI #34 (7 mm)

gathered rose—gather YLI #157 with 1 strand DMC #3713

lazy daisy leaves—YLI #155

large buds—2 Japanese ribbon stitches
- larger bottom stitch, YLI #34 (7 mm)
- smaller top stitch, YLI #157 (4 mm)

pearls

Paige: Template B for square-necked silk dress
Enlarge at 167%

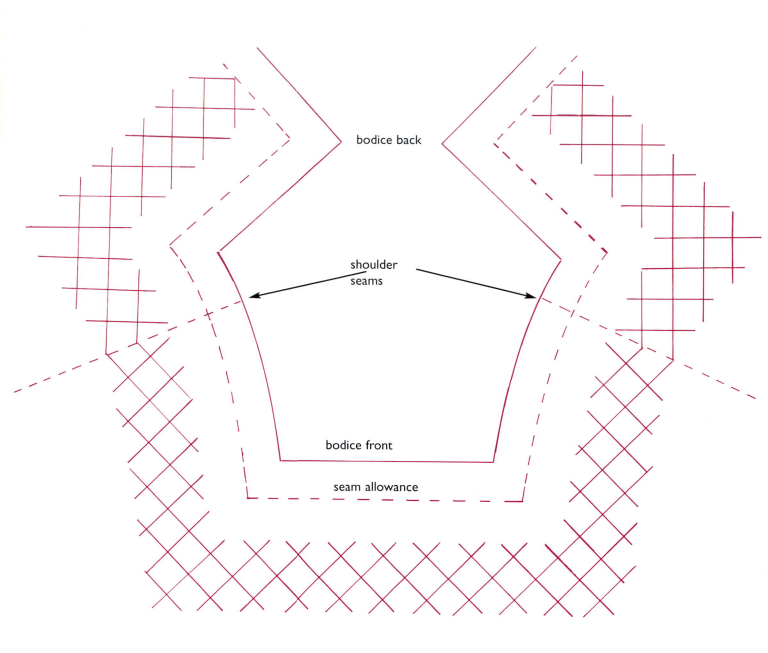

bodice back

shoulder
seams

bodice front

seam allowance

Paige: Template C for fringed shawl
pattern repeat

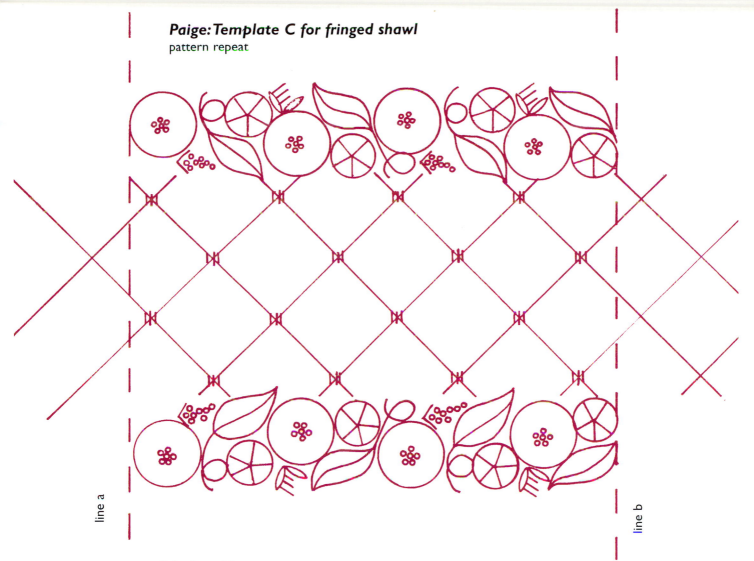

line a

line b

Stitch guide
(all stitches, I strand wool unless otherwise noted)

split stitch, Appleton #951
3 straight stitches; alternate Appleton #354 and Appleton #892

daisy
- centre—Appleton #331, 6 French knots, 2 twists each
- petals—Appleton #891, 12 decorative lazy daisy stitches

spider-web rose
- base—Appleton # 461
- weaving—I strand each Appleton #461 and #892

leaf
- stem and centre line—-outline stitch, Appleton #354
- sides of leaves—-straight stitches, Appleton #541 and #951
  (alternate top and bottom colour from leaf to leaf)

small bloom
- base—2 lazy daisy stitches, Appleton #353
- petals—3 straight stitches, Appleton #203

berries
- base—fly stitch, Appleton #353
- berries—seed stitch, Appleton #893

Paige: Template D for organdie party dress
pattern repeat

line a

line b

Stitch guide
(all stitches, 1 strand DMC floss unless otherwise noted)

daisy
- centre—6 French knots, 2 twists each, DMC #3821
- petals—12 decorative lazy daisy stitches, DMC white

bullion rose
- centre—DMC #725, 2 bullions, 6 wraps each; surrounded by 2 bullions with 10 and 13 wraps each
- outer petals—DMC #745, 8 bullions, 18 wraps each

leaf—shadow work, DMC #704

trellis—chain stitch, alternating rows of DMC #368, #471 and #704

tiny flowers
- base—2 decorative lazy daisy leaves, DMC #368
- blooms—3 feather stitches, DMC white; 1 French knot inside feather stitch, DMC #445, 3 twists

3 French knots, DMC #726, 2 strands, 3 twists

Virginia

Built around images symbolic of the sacrament of communion, and named after the woman who commissioned and constructed them, the 'Virginia' series of designs was created for First United Methodist Church of Tuscaloosa, Alabama, in 1997. Wheat stalks and grapevines form a cross in the central motif, and the smaller designs deconstruct that theme, as they focus closer and closer on the grape and the grain. The cross decorates the largest altar cloth, intended for the pulpit. A circle of grapevines and a sheaf of wheat are used on a pair of medium-sized altar scarves, and a grape bunch and three bound wheat stalks are designed for a pair of bookmarks intended to decorate a lectern. All the pieces were made from Ulster table linens in a unique project spearheaded by my friend Virginia Cade. Taken together, they form a wonderful project for an altar guild or a group of churchwomen who would enjoy creating a gift for their sanctuary.

TRANSFER

One hemstitched table runner was used to create the pulpit hanging, and the other cloths were cut from a large hemstitched tablecloth. There was a 2 inch (5 cm) border around the edge of the cloth, and the pieces were cut in such a way that each had a portion of this border across its bottom edge. All transfer was done with a water-soluble marker before construction and was washed away afterward, since the fabric takes laundering beautifully.

EMBROIDERY

A traditional ecru on white was the colour scheme Virginia and I wanted to work with so that the altar cloths could be used for communion services during any season of the church year. But the DMC colour called 'ecru' did not show up on the white background when viewed from the distances within our sanctuary. We tested several deeper beiges and chose the one used here because it echoed the golden cast of the interior wall colour. When I embroidered a tablecloth in this design for another sanctuary, I chose a different shade because its walls were a rosy beige. The best way to choose the right colour for your purpose is to take skeins of several beiges into the room where the altar hangings will be used and select the one which best complements its walls.

These designs call for a lot of satin stitch. As you embroider the right-angled cross, it will be important that you keep your stitches straight. The weave of the fabric will your best guide in doing this. There are several bunches of grapes which are also satin-stitched, and you will want to be sure that each grape is stitched in the same direction. For those on the cross and the narrow

Virginia pulpit scarf, richly embroidered in beige on white

lectern piece, that should be a vertical direction. On the altar scarves, where the grapes are in a circle, just be sure that all the grapes in the same bunch are worked in the same direction. Again, use the weave of the fabric to help you in your alignment. This will create a neater, more organised feel to the finished embroidery.

PULPIT SCARF
ILLUSTRATED OPPOSITE

Materials
18 x 48 inch (45 x 122 cm) table runner with 2 inch (5 cm) hemstitched band
3½ inch (9 cm) Cluny lace edging, 1⅓ yds (1.25 m)
¾ yd (70 cm) medium-weight interfacing
DMC cotton floss #739, 2 skeins
template A

Special embroidery notes
Positioning the template on the centre line of the fabric, 2¾ inch (7 cm) up from the line of hemstitching, and trace only the right-angled, basic cross form onto one end of the runner. Use a single strand of floss in a back stitch to outline it, starting at the bottom left-hand corner of the shape, but following the weave of the fabric instead of your markings. This will make your angles sharper and ensure that the design is truly straight and properly aligned with the fabric. Both arms should be ¾ inch (18 mm) wide, with the horizontal arm being 2½ inches (6.5 cm) long and the vertical arm 7 inches (17.5 cm) long. If the shape you outline doesn't exactly conform to the one you drew, don't worry—the new one is better. Remove your original markings, let the fabric dry, starch and press it. Now place the fabric over the template again, properly positioning the outlined shape over the corresponding area of the template. Transfer the rest of the design.

Follow the stitch guide carefully and work in this order:
- Satin-stitch the grapes at the centre of the cross; see stitch guide.
- With a single strand of floss, back-stitch the inner edges of the satin stitch border of the cross and use the same stitch to fill in the open space.
- Satin-stitch the border, fitting your stitches around the grapes where necessary.
- Using the weave of your fabric as a guide again, make the 5 vertical rows of evenly spaced seed stitches inside the border on the long vertical arm of the cross. Use 1 strand of floss, cover 3 woven threads in the linen, repeat the stitch 4 times in place, and leave 3 strands of woven linen vertically between each seed, as shown in the diagram on page 130.
- Make 5 horizontal rows of seed stitches inside the two horizontal arms in the same manner.
- Make the twining vine in outline stitch.
- Embroider the other grape bunches as you did the first.
- Embroider the curling tendrils and the leaves on each bunch in outline stitch.
- Embroider an outline stitch along the line which forms the triple-headed cap at the end of each arm.
- Make the wheat stems within the caps using outline stitch.
- Fill in the oval heads of the wheat using a fishbone stitch and ending each with one straight stitch at the tip.

Construction notes
You will need to interface the area inside the hemstitching to give it enough weight to hang properly. (As the border is already a doubled thickness of fabric it will not require any lining.) For this purpose cut a piece of interfacing the width of the runner within the hemstitched sides and half the runner's length, minus the hemstitched borders. Baste the interfacing to the wrong side of the unembroidered end. Using very small stitches, sew it in place as close to the hemstitching as possible down both of the runner's long sides. Fold the runner in half, wrong sides together, and whip the edges together all the way around. Whip the

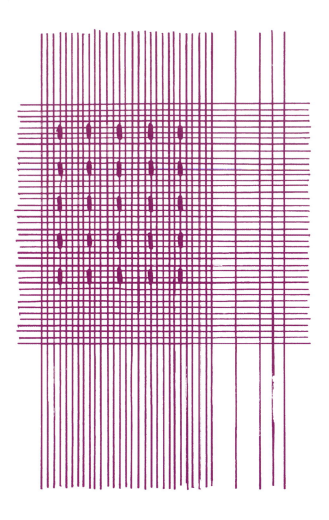

Detail of the central area of the cross embroidered with seed stitch. Each seed stitch covers 3 strands of the weave, and there are 3 woven strands (vertically) between each stitch. The number of strands between each stitch horizontally is not drawn to scale, but space the 5 rows of stitches evenly, as shown here.

hemstitching of the two layers together as well at intervals all the way around to provide stability.

To avoid any possible fraying edges, the lace trim on the end was doubled and seamed. First cut a length of lace which is twice the width of the finished altar cloth, plus 1 inch (2.5 cm). Before you cut the lace, make sure that you can align the pattern repeat when the lace is folded in half. Fold it in half with right sides together, and seam it at the open side with a ½ inch (12 mm) seam. Turn it right side out, press, and tack it together at intervals to create the look of a single layer. Attach it to the bottom edge of the pulpit scarf.

ALTAR SCARVES
ILLUSTRATED ON PAGE **131** AND PAGE **133**

Materials
white linen tablecloth with 2 inch (5 cm) hemstitched band; a cloth measuring 66 x 86 inches (168 x 220 cm) was sufficient for the altar scarves and the bookmarks
3½ inch (9 cm) Cluny lace edging, 1⅓ yd (1.25 m)
⅔ yd (60 cm) medium-weight interfacing
DMC cotton floss #739, 1 skein
templates B and C

Wheat sheaf motif from one of the Virginia altar scarves

Special embroidery notes

These scarves have finished measurements, with lace, of 32 x 8½ inches (81 x 21.5 cm). They are draped at each end of a rectangular altar table to coordinate with the hanging used on the pulpit. The size was determined to fit our particular altar and is not any ecclesiastical standard. If you plan to attach lace edging to the ends of your pieces, you should consider the length of the repeat in the lace pattern and use a multiple of that number for the width of the scarves so that the lace will fit neatly. Add a seam allowance to both sides of your pattern piece. For two scarves, you will need to cut this piece out four times, positioning it on the tablecloth each time so that it has a hemstitched border at its end. Zigzag all raw edges. Position the embroidery templates along the centre line of each scarf, having the lowest grape 2¾ inches (7 cm) above the line of hemstitching and the wheat sheaf 2 inches (5 cm) above the line. Transfer the designs with a water-soluble marking pen.

There is no particular order for the embroidery on the scarf with the grapevine circle. Just follow the stitch guide. On the wheat-embellished scarf, I found it easiest to do the satin-stitched ribbons first and then to fit the stalks of the wheat up to them. Lastly embroider the heads of the wheat as the stitch guide instructs.

Construction notes

Cut two pieces of interfacing by the same method used for the pulpit scarf, and baste one to the wrong side of each embroidered piece. Place the right side of each scarf to the right side of a corresponding lining piece and stitch along the side seam lines, starting at the bottom of the hemstitched band and sewing up one long side, across the plain end, and down the other long side. Leave the hemstitched end open. Turn right sides out and press. See the construction notes for the pulpit scarf for instructions for creating the lace edging. Whip the edging to the hemstitched end of the scarf, stitching both pieces of linen together at the same time. For stability, tack the hemstitching of the two pieces together at intervals also.

BOOKMARKS
ILLUSTRATED ON PAGE 132

Materials
white linen tablecloth or table runner with 2 inch
  (5 cm) hemstitched band
3½ inch (9 cm) Cluny lace edging, ⅔ yd (60 cm)
⅔ yd (60 cm) medium-weight interfacing
DMC cotton floss:
  #739, 1 skein
templates D and E

Left Grape motif from Virginia bookmarks (see page 132)
Right Wheat motif from Virginia bookmarks

Special embroidery notes

These narrow pieces measure, when finished with lace, 33 x 3½ inches (84 x 9 cm). See the special embroidery notes for the altar scarves for pattern and cutting instructions. Position the embroidery templates on the centre line of each bookmark 4¼ inches (11 cm) above the line of hemstitching and trace with a water-soluble marker.

On the wheat motif, embroider the stems first. For the rest of the work, there is no particular order to follow. Refer to the stitch guide for directions.

Construction notes

See construction notes for altar scarves.

Bonus idea

The cross is a lovely design for the front panel or bodice of a first communion dress. Reduce the size and embroider it on handkerchief-weight linen or batiste in shadow work, ecru on white.

The grapevine motif from one of the Virginia altar scarves (see page 130)

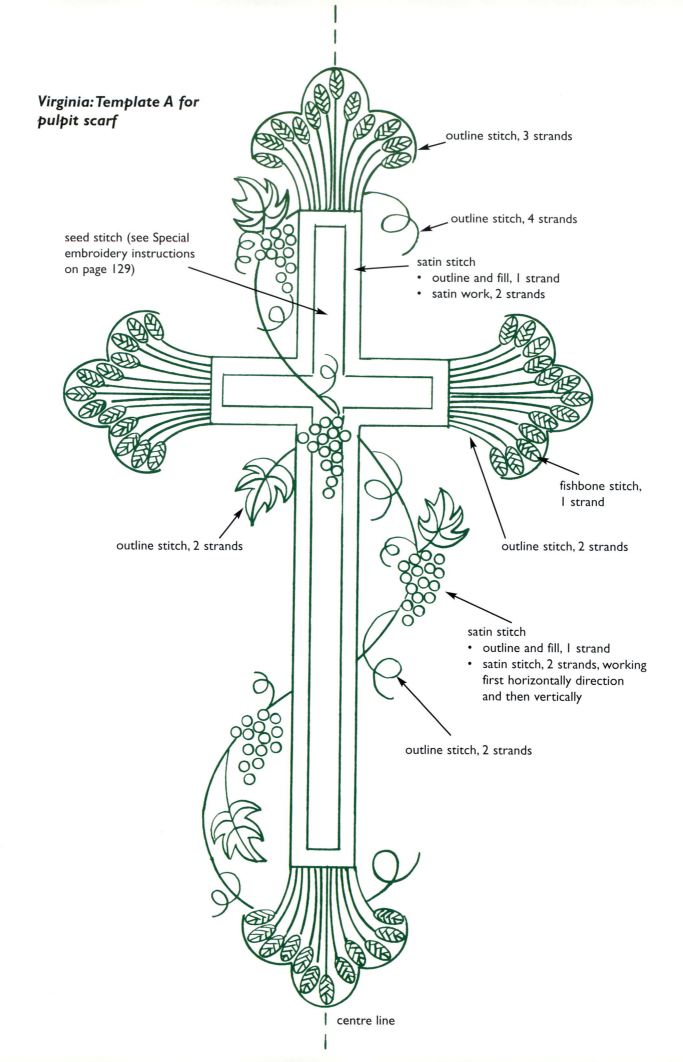

Virginia: Template A for pulpit scarf

outline stitch, 3 strands

outline stitch, 4 strands

satin stitch
- outline and fill, 1 strand
- satin work, 2 strands

seed stitch (see Special embroidery instructions on page 129)

fishbone stitch, 1 strand

outline stitch, 2 strands

outline stitch, 2 strands

satin stitch
- outline and fill, 1 strand
- satin stitch, 2 strands, working first horizontally direction and then vertically

outline stitch, 2 strands

centre line

Virginia: Template B for altar scarf (grape vine)

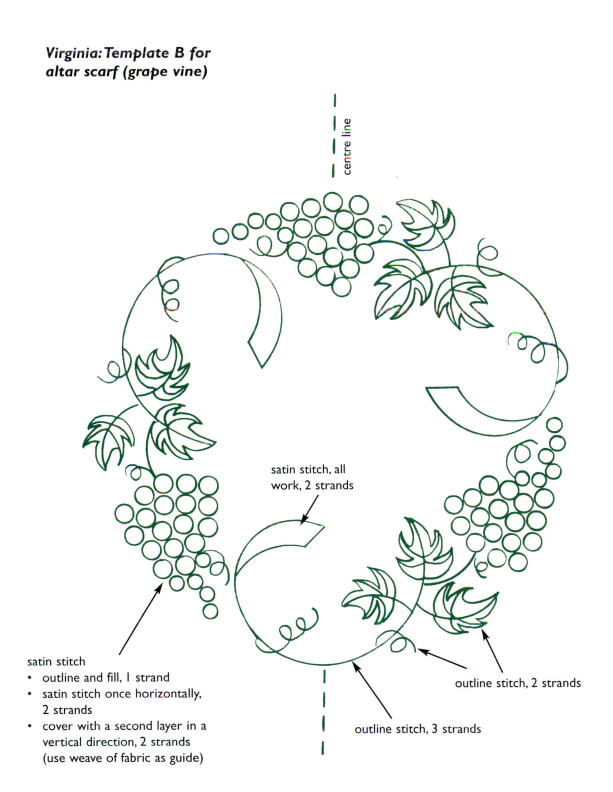

centre line

satin stitch, all
work, 2 strands

satin stitch
- outline and fill, 1 strand
- satin stitch once horizontally, 2 strands
- cover with a second layer in a vertical direction, 2 strands (use weave of fabric as guide)

outline stitch, 2 strands

outline stitch, 3 strands

**Virginia: Template C for
altar scarf (wheat sheaf)**

centre line

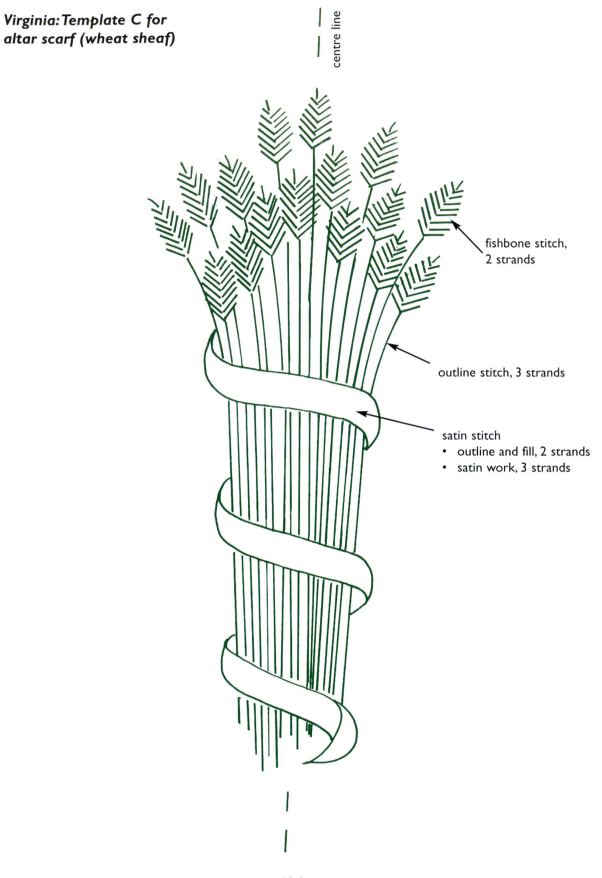

fishbone stitch,
2 strands

outline stitch, 3 strands

satin stitch
• outline and fill, 2 strands
• satin work, 3 strands

**Virginia: Template D for
bookmark (wheat motif)**

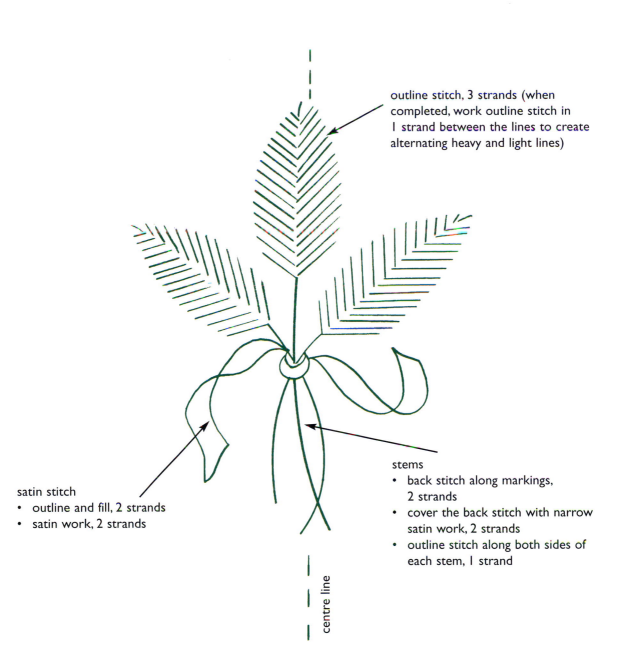

outline stitch, 3 strands (when
completed, work outline stitch in
1 strand between the lines to create
alternating heavy and light lines)

satin stitch
• outline and fill, **2** strands
• satin work, 2 strands

stems
• back stitch along markings,
  2 strands
• cover the back stitch with narrow
  satin work, 2 strands
• outline stitch along both sides of
  each stem, 1 strand

centre line

Virginia: Template E for bookmark (grape motif)

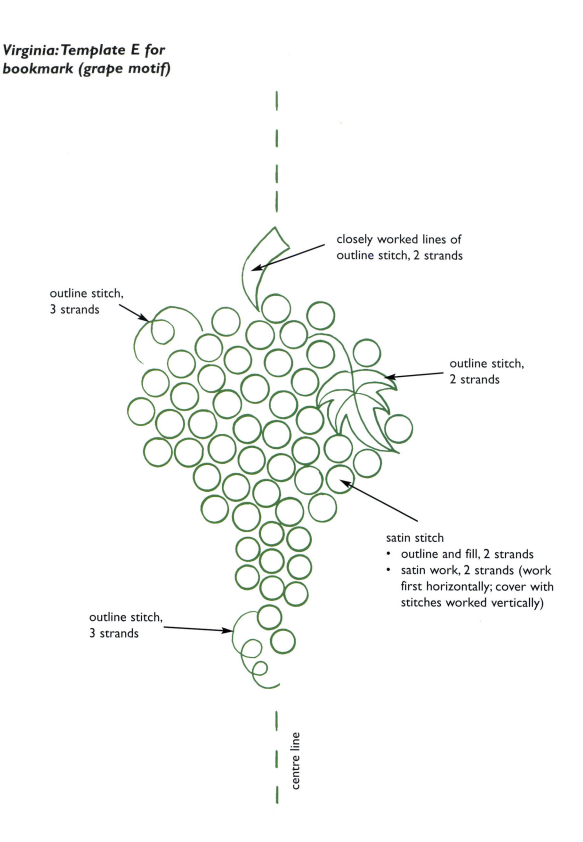

closely worked lines of outline stitch, 2 strands

outline stitch, 3 strands

outline stitch, 2 strands

satin stitch
- outline and fill, 2 strands
- satin work, 2 strands (work first horizontally; cover with stitches worked vertically)

outline stitch, 3 strands

centre line

This medallion-style oval topped off with a flowing bow is an excellent device for creating a focal point wherever you need one. Used on its flower-studded background or standing alone, it is sure to attract attention. Its versatility is highlighted in the three projects illustrated—you will find it worked in traditional floss on the bodice of a child's dress, in silk ribbon and beads on a formal gown, and worked in shadow embroidery on a sheer window hanging.

TRANSFER

Mark and embroider each of the three projects before constructing them. Some alterations are made to the bodice of the child's dress and to the window hanging before marking (see Special embroidery notes). The dress treatment and the window treatment can be traced from their templates with water-soluble markers, as they are worked on white cotton or linen. The ribbon-embroidery design, on a heavy satin bodice, was traced from the template using a purple disappearing marker. The design is not large and can be worked at one sitting, reducing the inconvenience of having it fade out. If necessary, the markings for the background beading can be done separately from the central motif. You will need to assemble the three pattern pieces which form the bodice before transferring the design.

EMBROIDERY

Embroider the flower stems and the oval first since some of the flowers overlap or abut them. Fill in the blossoms and foliage next, saving the background French knots or beads for last.

GIRL'S EMPIRE DRESS
ILLUSTRATED ON PAGE 140

Materials

Children's Corner pattern, 'Marilyn', view B
white cotton sateen
pale blue cotton sateen for contrast trim
DMC cotton floss:
   #369, green
   #761, pink
   #775, blue (may vary to match blue sateen fabric)
   #818, pale pink
templates A and B

Special embroidery notes

The 'Marilyn' bodice has an asymmetrical focal point which doesn't suit a centred motif and must be altered. To do this, fold the yoke overlay pattern piece vertically down a centre line, matching up the armholes. Fold in half a sheet of tracing paper large enough for that pattern piece. Aligning the folded edges of the two, lay the tracing paper on top of the folded yoke, which is turned so that the wearer's left side (the side with the v at the bottom edge) is showing. Trace only

that side onto the paper. Putting aside the original yoke overlay, turn the tracing paper over and trace an identical right side. Open out the new yoke overlay and round out the centre bottom curve. Centre template A on the new pattern piece and trace. Transfer the entire new bodice with its design onto your fabric. Reshape the yoke overlay band using the same method.

Template B is a repeat for the French knot decoration on the sleeves and should be large enough to accommodate all pattern sizes. Centre the sleeve pattern over it and trace onto the paper, then transfer to the fabric. Do the same for the bodice.

The embroidery here relies on basic stitches and is fairly simple, but the pink blossoms may be a new twist on an old idea for you. The daisy-like blooms are formed by making two overlapping rings of lazy daisy stitches. Make the outer ring of pale pink stitches first, starting each stitch on the inner circle and ending on the outer one. The second set of stitches is done in the darker pink and overlaps the first. Each stitch starts from the centre of the small oval and extends just past its outer edge to cover the base of the first set of lazy daisies. You will have about half as many stitches in that ring as you had in the outer circle. Follow the stitch guide for the rest of the embroidery.

Construction notes
Follow pattern instructions.

FORMAL GOWN
ILLUSTRATED ON PAGE 142

Materials
McCall's pattern #9225, view A
taupe heavy satin
gold silk faille, ½ yd (0.5 m), for contrast band
⅜ inch (8 mm) cording, 1 yd (1 m)
Mill Hill glass seed beads, 1 pack each:
    #02019, honey
    #02010, ice

YLI ribbon (4 mm):
    #87, blush
    #88, terra cotta
    #164, taupe
YLI ribbon (7 mm):
    #56, olive green
DMC cotton floss:
    #640, taupe
    #783, gold
templates B and C

Special embroidery notes
Following the stitch guides with templates B and C start your embroidery with the stems of the gold flowers using 2 strands of taupe floss in outline stitch. Each stem ends in a fly stitch, which forms a base for a gold bloom. The blooms are made of the honey seed beads attached with gold floss. Don't worry about exact placement of each bead; just make sure the bloom ends up being the same general shape as that in the template. Tie off your thread after each bead to avoid losing them all if one should pull loose. It will not be necessary to cut the thread until all the beads in a cluster have been attached.

Make the oval next, using taupe ribbon in outline stitch. Cut five 8 inch (20 cm) strands of the same colour to make the bow. All five begin at approximately the same point near the top of the oval. Three of them form loose loops ending back near the starting point, the other two are the free ends. Twist the ribbon to form the folds indicated on the template by an ×. Pin and tack each in place with the taupe floss and a clear ice bead where indicated. Cover the centre spot where all the stitches converge with a bead.

The oval-shaped pink blossoms are formed from Japanese ribbon stitches. Begin with an outer ring of lighter pink in which the stitches start from the edge of the inner circle and extend to the edge of the outer circle. Place 3 ribbon stitches of darker pink on top of them, beginning from the centre and extending out to just overlap the bases of the bottom layer stitches. Use gold

Opposite Wendy girl's empire dress embroidered in cotton floss

Detail of bodice embroidery in cotton floss on girl's empire dress

floss to attach 3 honey seed beads in each centre atop the darker pink petals. Each green leaf is 1 Japanese ribbon stitch in wide ribbon.

The background motif is simply a scattering of flower-shaped clusters of clear ice beads. Attach them with the taupe floss used for the flower stems.

Construction notes

A finished satin lining was constructed for the dress bodice, rather than one made from lining fabric as called for by the dress pattern. To do this, cut two identical satin bodices—one you will embroider, the other you will apply interfacing to. Then attach the straps as the pattern directs and join the two bodices, with right sides together, at the top, side and underarm seams. Trim, clip and press the seams open, and turn the bodice right side out. All raw edges will be between the bodice and its lining.

To create the decorative trim at the waistline, cut and assemble 1 yard (1 m) of 2¼ inch (5.75 cm)

Opposite Wendy formal gown (see previous page)

wide bias strips of gold faille. Fold the yardage in half lengthwise to loosely cover the cording. Insert into the waistline seam to form a decorative band ½ inch (12 mm) wide.

WINDOW HANGING
MATERIALS
Vogue pattern #2243, view B-7
pink organza; double the pattern yardage and add
  ½ yd (0.5 m) for valance
handkerchief linen; add ⅓ yd (30 cm) to pattern
  yardage for valance contrast overlay
DMC floss:
  #224, salmon
  #3023, taupe
  #3046, gold
  #3364, green
template D

Special embroidery notes

This sheer window hanging is designed for use on a French door and may be used singly or in a pair. The embroidery is done on the linen contrast overlay of a valance which does not appear in the pattern, but is simple to create. Following the pattern's sewing instructions for view B, cut two full-length panels of the organza fabric (the organza panel will hang better when doubled) and one of the linen contrast. Note that the contrast panel is narrower than the fabric panel. Using guide 7 as the sewing instructions illustrate, cut the tapered ends of those panels. For the valance, use guide 7 literally as a pattern piece to cut two 19 inch (48 cm) long panels of the organza fabric. Fold the top of the guide down 3 inches (8 cm) to shorten it and cut one 16 inch (40 cm) long contrast panel out of linen, noting the pattern markings as to its width. This is the piece you will mark with template D for your embroidery. Follow pattern instructions for finishing its edges before you begin the embroidery to avoid stretching and fraying. Use 2 strands of floss for the large-scale shadow embroidery and complete according to the stitch guide.

Wendy window hanging of pink organza, finished with a handkerchief linen valance embroidered in shadow work (see page 143)

Construction notes

Finish the edges of the long linen overlay as you did the valance overlay. Pin the two long organza panels right sides together, stitch, turn and press. Do the same for the organza valance. Centre and pin the wrong side of the long linen overlay to the right side of the long organza panel. Baste the raw edges together. Do the same for the valance.

Pin the right side of the valance to the wrong side of the curtain and stitch along the seam line. Press the seam open and finish the raw edges. Turn right side out and drape over curtain rod. The drapery can be hot-glued into place or, if you prefer a rod casing, create one by simply stitching through all thicknesses of the curtain 2½ inches (6.5 cm) from the top, and insert the rod.

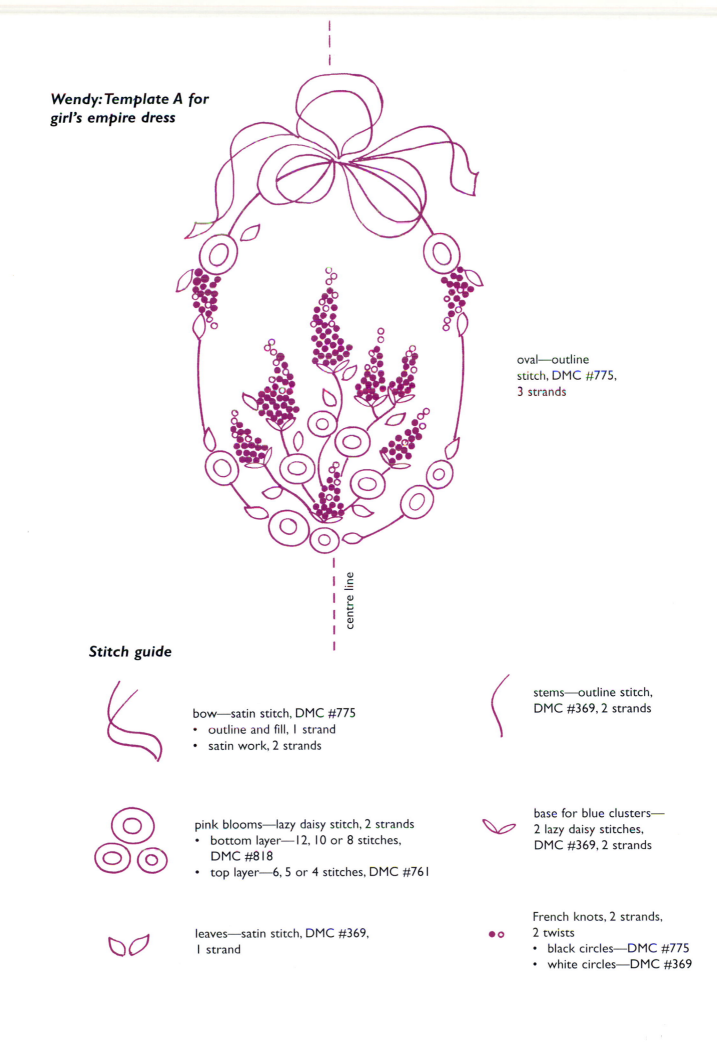

Wendy: Template A for girl's empire dress

oval—outline stitch, DMC #775, 3 strands

centre line

Stitch guide

bow—satin stitch, DMC #775
- outline and fill, 1 strand
- satin work, 2 strands

stems—outline stitch, DMC #369, 2 strands

pink blooms—lazy daisy stitch, 2 strands
- bottom layer—12, 10 or 8 stitches, DMC #818
- top layer—6, 5 or 4 stitches, DMC #761

base for blue clusters— 2 lazy daisy stitches, DMC #369, 2 strands

leaves—satin stitch, DMC #369, 1 strand

French knots, 2 strands, 2 twists
- black circles—DMC #775
- white circles—DMC #369

Wendy: Template B

Background motif for use with templates A and C

- for child's dress bodice and sleeves, French knots
  DMC #775, 2 strands, 3 twists
- for formal gown bodice, attach #02010 seed
  beads with DMC #640, 1 strand

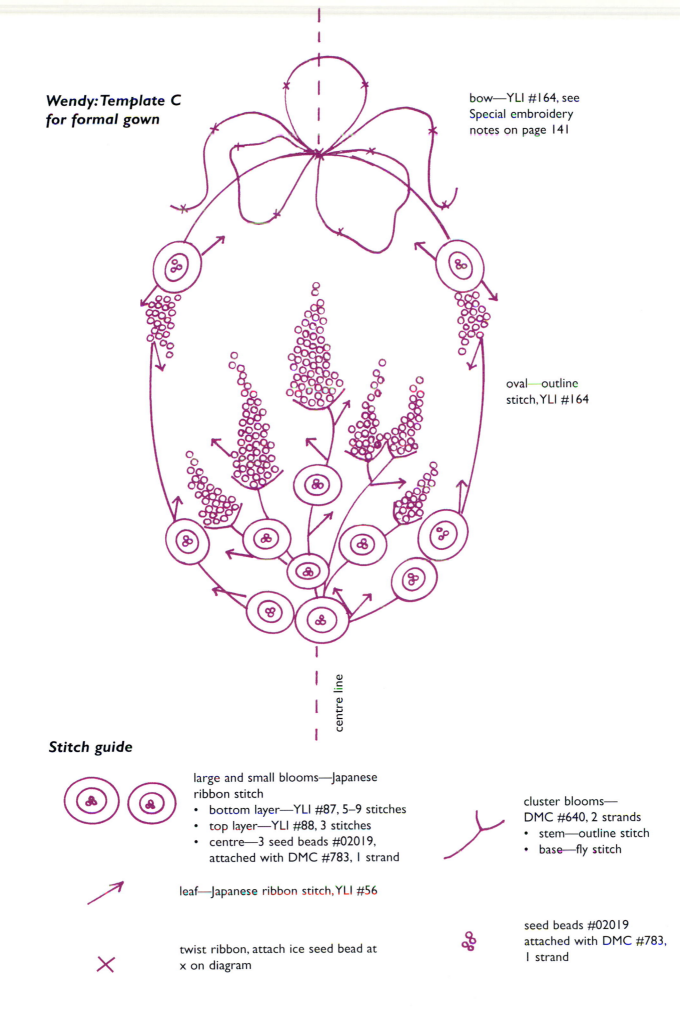

Wendy: Template C for formal gown

bow—YLI #164, see Special embroidery notes on page 141

oval—outline stitch, YLI #164

centre line

Stitch guide

large and small blooms—Japanese ribbon stitch
- bottom layer—YLI #87, 5–9 stitches
- top layer—YLI #88, 3 stitches
- centre—3 seed beads #02019, attached with DMC #783, 1 strand

leaf—Japanese ribbon stitch, YLI #56

twist ribbon, attach ice seed bead at x on diagram

cluster blooms—DMC #640, 2 strands
- stem—outline stitch
- base—fly stitch

seed beads #02019 attached with DMC #783, 1 strand

Wendy: Template D for window hanging
See stitch guide on page 143

stems—outline stitch,
DMC #3023, 2 strands

oval—chain stitch,
DMC #3023, I strand

centre line

Wendy: Stitch guide for Template D

bow
- shadow work—DMC #224, I strand
- accent—DMC #224, outline stitch, 2 strands

roses
- centres—DMC #224, 2 bullions, 9 wraps each, 2 strands
- outer petals—shadow work, DMC #224, 2 strands

cluster blooms, leaves and bases—shadow work, DMC # 3364, I strand

cluster blooms
- white circles, DMC #224, shadow work, I strand
- black circles, DMC #3046, shadow work, I strand

Suppliers

Ready-made items shown in this book were sourced from the following US suppliers.

Aislinn
Page 37—Rectangular flanged boudoir pillow—Ulster Weaving

Blair
Page 47—Tatted insertion and Cluny lace—Boutros Imports
Page 51—White organdie shower curtain—Garnet Hill, Inc.

Carolyn
Page 59—Black velveteen purse—Gap
Page 61—Child's jacket and cap—Land's End

Claire
Page 68—Tatting—Boutros Imports
Page 69—Tatting and Battenburg lace—Boutros Imports

Gerry
Page 91—Vintage Garden silk fleece throw—JLA Home, Inc.

Virginia
Page 129, 130—Table runner and table cloth—Ulster Weaving
Page 130—Cluny lace—Boutros Imports

Resources

Appleton Brothers, Church Street, Chiswick, London W42E, England
Call 0181 994-0711
For wool threads

Bear Threads, 5690 West Princeton Dr., Denver, CO, USA 80235
Call (303) 619-7420
www.bearthreads.com
For fine heirloom fabrics

Boutros Imports, 209 25th St, Brooklyn, NY, USA 11232
Call (800) 227-7781
For fine linens and laces ('Aislinn', 'Blair', 'Claire', 'Virginia')

Bucilla
Call (800) 842-4197
www.bucilla.com
For silk ribbon ('Blair', 'Gerry')

Butterick Patterns
USA, call (800) 766-3619, ext. 488
Outside USA, call Intl. access code
+ 1 (785) 776-4041, ext. 488
www.butterick.com
For garment and home sewing patterns ('Carolyn')

Chery Williams Patterns, PO Box 190234, Birmingham, AL, USA 35219
For quality children's heirloom patterns ('Adrienne', 'Aislinn', 'Claire, 'Evers', 'Miriam')

Clover Needlecraft, Inc., 1007 East Dominguez St, Suite L, Carson, CA, USA 90746-3620
Email: clovercni@earthlink.net
For needlework accessories ('Miriam')

Creative Publishing, Intl.
Singer Sewing Reference Library, Sewing Instructions for the Home, published 1991
Call (800) 328-3895
www.creativepublishinginternational.com
('Evers')

DMC
www.dmc.com
For embroidery flosses

Foxgloves Alley, 511 15th St, Tuscaloosa, AL, USA 35401
Call (205) 752-9387
Retail outlet for fine cotton, silk, and wool threads and needlepoint supplies

Gap
Call (888) 906-1104
www.gap.com
For accessories ('Carolyn')

Garnet Hill, Inc., 231 Main St, Franconia, NH, USA 03580
USA, call (800) 870-3513
Outside USA, call Intl. access code
+ 1 (603) 823-5545
www.garnethill.com
Natural fibre clothing and linens ('Blair')

JLA Home Inc, 19410 Cabot Blvd, Hayward, CA, USA 94545
Call (888) 888-8552
www.jlahome.com
For silk blankets ('Gerry')

Land's End, Land's End Lane, Dodgerville, WI, USA 53595
USA and Canada, call (800) 963-4816
All other countries, call Intl. access code + 1
(608) 935-6170
www.landsend.com
For outer wear ('Carolyn')

Mill Hill, PO Box 1060, Janesville, WI, USA 53547
www.millhill.com
For beads ('Wendy')

Sarah Howard Stone, Inc., 2754 Boultier St, Montgomery, AL, USA, 36106
French Hand Sewing for Infants, by Sarah
Howard Stone, published 1984
www.sarahhowardstone.com
('Lauren')

Sew So Fancy, 914 Queen City Ave, Tuscaloosa, AL, USA 35401
Call (800) 821-0607
Retail outlet for fine fabrics, laces, ribbons and flosses; garment construction and needlework classes; baby gifts and fine household linens

Simplicity Patterns
USA and Canada, call (888) 588-2700
UK and Europe, email:
simplicityuk@compuserve.com
Australia, email: simplicityoz@compuserve.com
For garment and home sewing patterns ('Paige')

Spechler-Vogel, 234 West 39th St, New York, NY, USA 10018
Call (800) 223-2031
For fine heirloom fabrics

Stylecrest Fabrics Ltd, 500 7th Ave, 6/Fl., New York, NY, USA 10018
Call (212) 354-0123
www.stylecrest.com
For fine dress fabrics

Terry Jane, Inc., c/o A.T. Newell Co., 451 South 64th Place, Birmingham, AL, USA 35212
For smocking plates ('Aislinn')

The Children's Corner, 3814 Cleghorn Ave, Nashville, TN, USA 37215
Call (800) 543-6915
www.childrenscornerfabric.com
For quality children's heirloom patterns ('Blair', 'Gerry', 'Wendy')

The McCall Pattern Co., 11 Penn Plaza, New York, NY, USA 10018
Call (800) 782-0323
www.mccall.com
For garment and home sewing patterns ('Adrienne', 'Paige', 'Wendy')

The Smocking Bird, 2904-B Linden Ave, Birmingham, AL, USA 35209
Call (205) 879-5502
www.thesmockingbird.com
Retail outlet for fine fabrics, laces, ribbons and flosses; garment construction and needlework classes; Bernina dealership

Ulster Weaving, 148 Madison Ave, New York, NY, USA 10016
Call (212) 684-5534
www.ulsterlinen.com
For fine linen fabrics and domestic linens ('Aislinn', 'Virginia')

Vogue Patterns
USA, call (800) 766-3619, ext. 488
Outside USA, call Intl. access code
+ 1 (785) 776-4041, ext. 488
www.voguepatterns.com
For garment and home sewing patterns ('Paige', 'Wendy')

YLI Corporation, 161 West Main St, Rock Hill, SC, USA 29730
Call (800) 296-8139
Email: ylicorp@rhtc.net
For silk embroidery ribbon